A Painter's Odyssey

The Art of Marshall Bouldin III

with essays by
Marshall Bouldin IV
Daniel Piersol

edited by
Robin C. Dietrick

MISSISSIPPI MUSEUM *of* ART
Jackson

At work in studio, circa 1971.

This book is made possible through the generous support of

Sherry Stribling Greener

with additional funding by

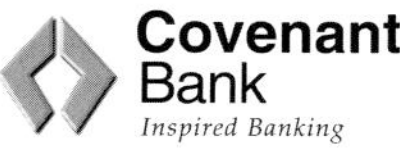

Mr. and Mrs. Penn Owen, Jr.
and the Brick Gallery, Clarksdale, Mississippi

The exhibition *A Painter's Odyssey: The Art of Marshall Bouldin III*, curated by Daniel Piersol, appeared at the Mississippi Museum of Art from September 20, 2008 through January 4, 2009.

The Mississippi Museum of Art and its programs are sponsored in part by the City of Jackson and the Jackson Convention & Visitors Bureau. Support is also provided in part by funding from the Mississippi Arts Commission, a state agency, and by the National Endowment for the Arts, a federal agency.

All artwork is from the collection of the artist, unless otherwise noted.

Artwork from the collection of the artist; the collection of the Russell C. Davis Planetarium, Jackson, Mississippi; the collection of Roman Catholic Diocese of Jackson, Mississippi; the collection of Mr. and Mrs. Freeman Randolph and Helen Bouldin Jones, Charlotte, North Carolina; and the collection of Mr. and Mrs. John Cooper, Jr., Bella Vista, Arkansas, was photographed by Bill Jackson, Gil Ford Photography.

Artwork from the collection of Mississippi Department of Archives and History, Jackson, was photographed by Tom Joynt.

Library of Congress
Cataloging-in-Publication Data

Bouldin, Marshall, 1923-
A painter's odyssey : the art of Marshall Bouldin III / with essays by Marshall Bouldin IV, Daniel Piersol ; edited by Robin C. Dietrick.
p. cm.
ISBN 978-1-887422-17-8
1. Bouldin, Marshall, 1923---Exhibitions. I. Bouldin, Marshall, 1960- II. Piersol, Daniel. III. Dietrick, Robin C., 1978- IV. Mississippi Museum of Art. V. Title.
ND1329.B68A4 2008
759.13--dc22
2008038800

Edited by Robin C. Dietrick.
Interview transcribed by George Eric McDonald.
Copyedited by Katie Blount.
Designed by Heidi Flynn Barnett, Flynn Design.
Printed in Canada by Friesens.

Mississippi Museum of Art

ISBN 978-1-887422-17-8

(Cover image)

Self-Portrait, 2006, oil on canvas, 9 x 6. *Collection of Mr. and Mrs. Freeman Randolph and Helen Bouldin Jones, Charlotte, North Carolina.*

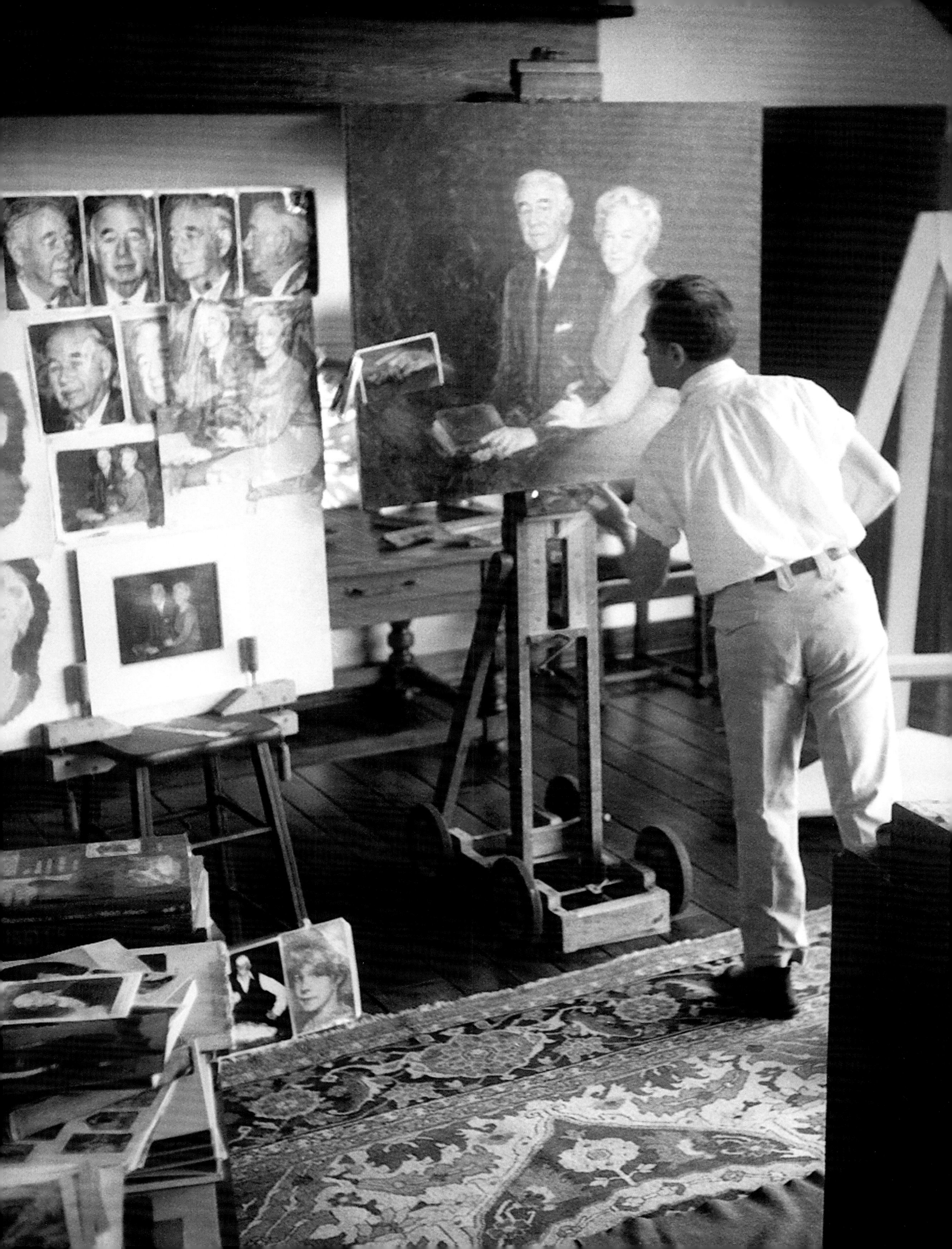

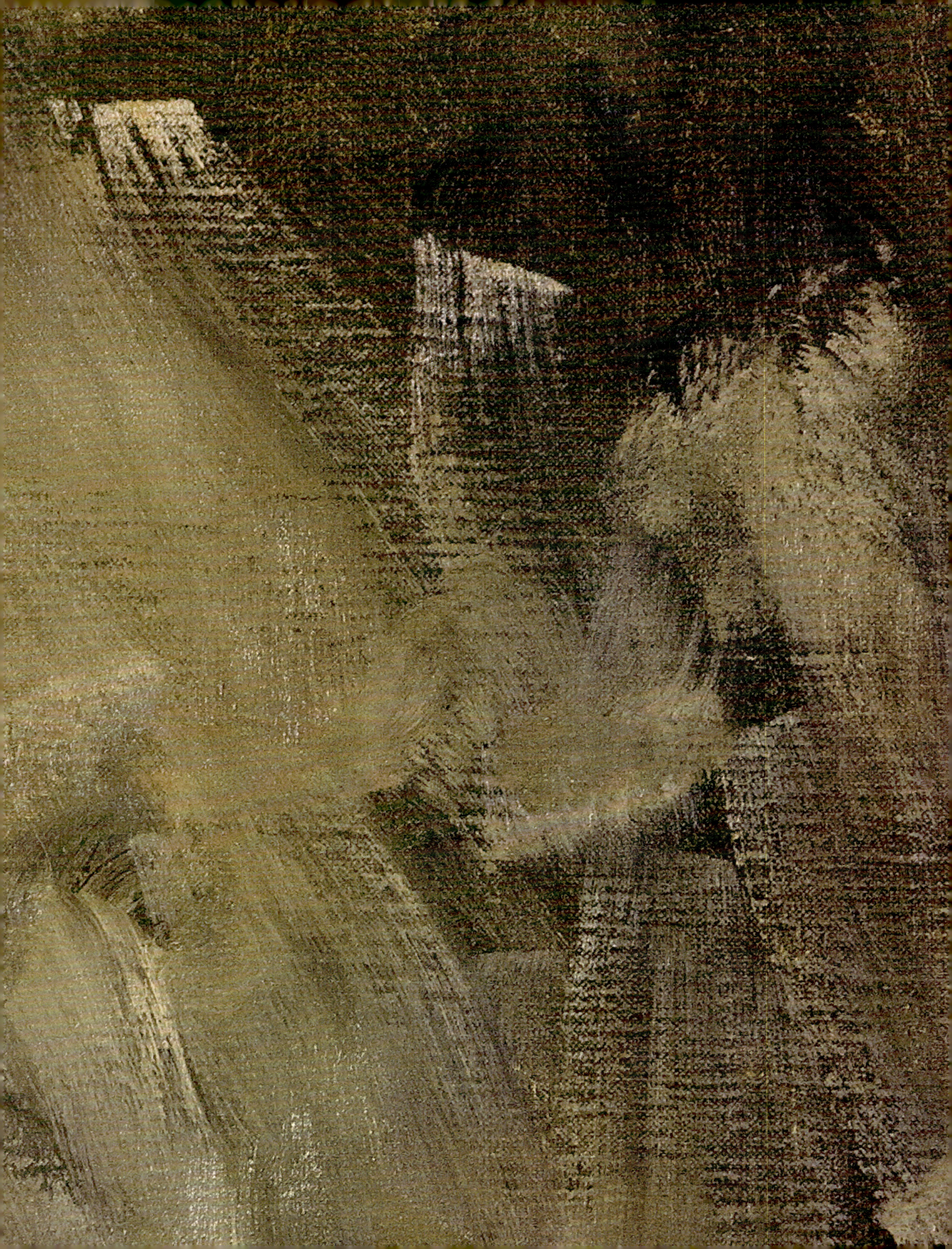

Contents

Foreword

In *One Writer's Beginnings*, Eudora Welty tells a story about the ubiquitous Sunday afternoon drive. She remembers positioning herself in the back seat of a car between her mother and a neighbor and instructing the ladies, "Now TALK!"

We all surely have similar memories of the sounds of our relatives' voices on those Sunday drives. I remember distinctly a Sunday drive with my grandparents in the countryside near Clarksdale. As we paused before an orchard they pointed down the lane to the home of their neighbor, a "famous artist." I was fascinated by the story of the painter, his physician wife, and the four little boys whom my grandmother taught at the Episcopal day school in town. Every now and then I would get updates: one of the boys is a Rhodes Scholar, another is painting like his father, another is a doctor like his mother, another frames the art and composes classical music. The generations of Bouldins in Coahoma County, Mississippi, run as deep as the roots of those trees through which I peeked, hoping to get a glimpse of a real artist. And the community's pride in Marshall Bouldin's successful career is deeper, still.

The time has come to recognize this devoted son of Mississippi, this loving patriarch, and one of the nation's most esteemed portrait painters of the second half of the 20th century. The Mississippi Museum of Art is honored to be the agent of that recognition, and we hope that this book offers an intimate look at one of our most serious and accomplished resident artists.

This project was inspired by Bouldin's son, student, apprentice, and fellow painter, Jason Bouldin, whose gentle but firm guidance helped insure the integrity and dignity of our exhibition and publication. Another son, Marshall IV, contributed a loving and eloquent essay about his father's work. Indeed the entire Bouldin family, including the artist himself and his wife, graciously allowed our curator, Dan Piersol, to linger with them, conduct interviews, and delight in the atmosphere that has spawned such creativity in the Delta. Robin Dietrick, the book's editor, and Heidi Barnett, the designer, captured the breadth and depth of this painter's career, creating a document that will illuminate Bouldin's work for generations to come. Other capable hands and minds contributed greatly to this work: Katie Blount, copyeditor; Maureen Donnelly, interview assistant; and George Eric McDonald, transcriber.

Though my grandparents are long gone, the Bouldin family continues to inspire admiration and devotion in their neighbors: this project has been generously supported by Clarksdale's Covenant Bank, Norma and Penn Owen, Jr., and the Brick Gallery; as well as Juniker Jewelry Co. and Gloria Walker, both of Jackson.

Finally, this book is a loving gift from Sherry Stribling Greener, who considers herself fortunate to be counted in the larger Bouldin family, and to whom the Museum is extremely grateful.

When Dan Piersol went to Clarksdale to interview Marshall Bouldin, all he needed to do was to recite Eudora Welty's instruction, "Now, TALK!" Our wish for you as you turn these pages is that you hear this great artist's gentle voice and see through his piercing eyes. If you do, you will find an incomparable record of the people, the places, and the expressions of our home and beyond.

BETSY BRADLEY
Director

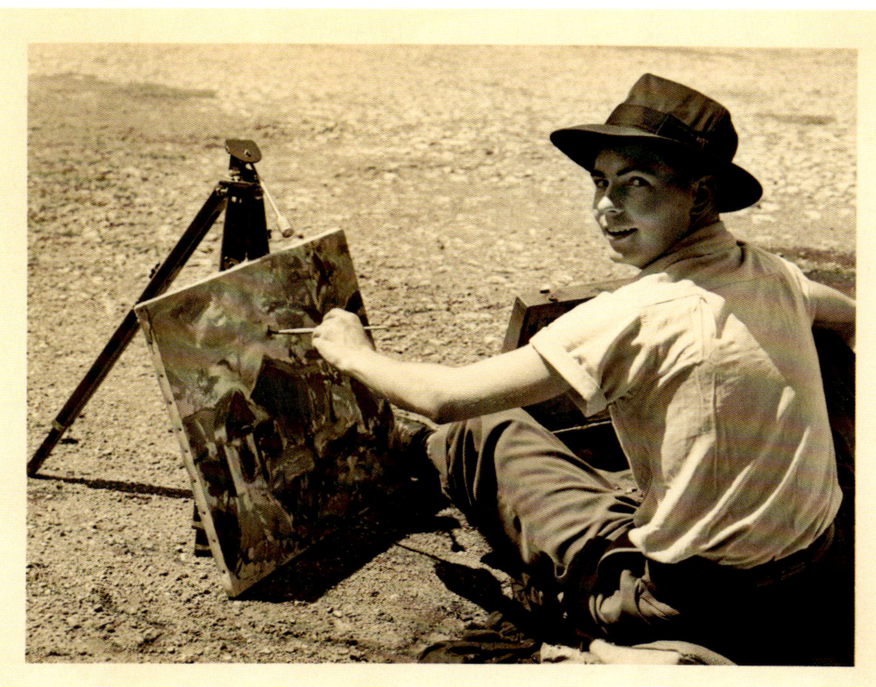

A young Marshall Bouldin III at work.

Working quietly for over six decades in a small Mississippi Delta town, Marshall Bouldin III has become the state's most celebrated and perhaps one of the nation's most successful portrait painters, with more than 800 commissions to his credit.

Bouldin has dedicated his life to his art, working in his studio every day, even on Sundays. His work ethic shows in his paintings, as does his care and attention to detail. Bouldin takes the time to get to know his subjects, their mannerisms and personalities. And it is the essence of the sitter that comes through in the artist's works. Any accomplished portrait artist can create a likeness of the subject, but Bouldin is able to magically capture a person's spirit in oil paint on canvas.

This book traces Bouldin's journey from the beginning, with each turn in the path revealing more clearly his calling as a portrait artist. Not an academic study of Bouldin's paintings, this is a more intimate look at the artist's life and work. First, Marshall Bouldin IV offers a thorough yet personal overview of his father's life. Daniel Piersol, Mississippi Museum of Art deputy director for programs, takes a more analytical approach, exploring Bouldin's work through the eyes of a museum professional. And finally, the artist himself looks back on his career, in a wide-ranging conversation with Piersol. These components of *A Painter's Odyssey* function as three variations on the theme of Marshall Bouldin.

Nearly forty of Bouldin's paintings are illustrated here, appearing along with a number of family photographs from the artist's personal archives. This private material allows the reader a closer look at the man behind the likenesses of so many people.

A Painter's Odyssey: The Art of Marshall Bouldin III is a long-overdue look at the life of an exceptional artist. Bouldin's spirituality and his dedication to his work are evident in the luminous works of art that come from his studio. Here, readers will discover how the passion developed and how he intends to keep channeling it for years to come.

Robin C. Dietrick
Editor

Introduction

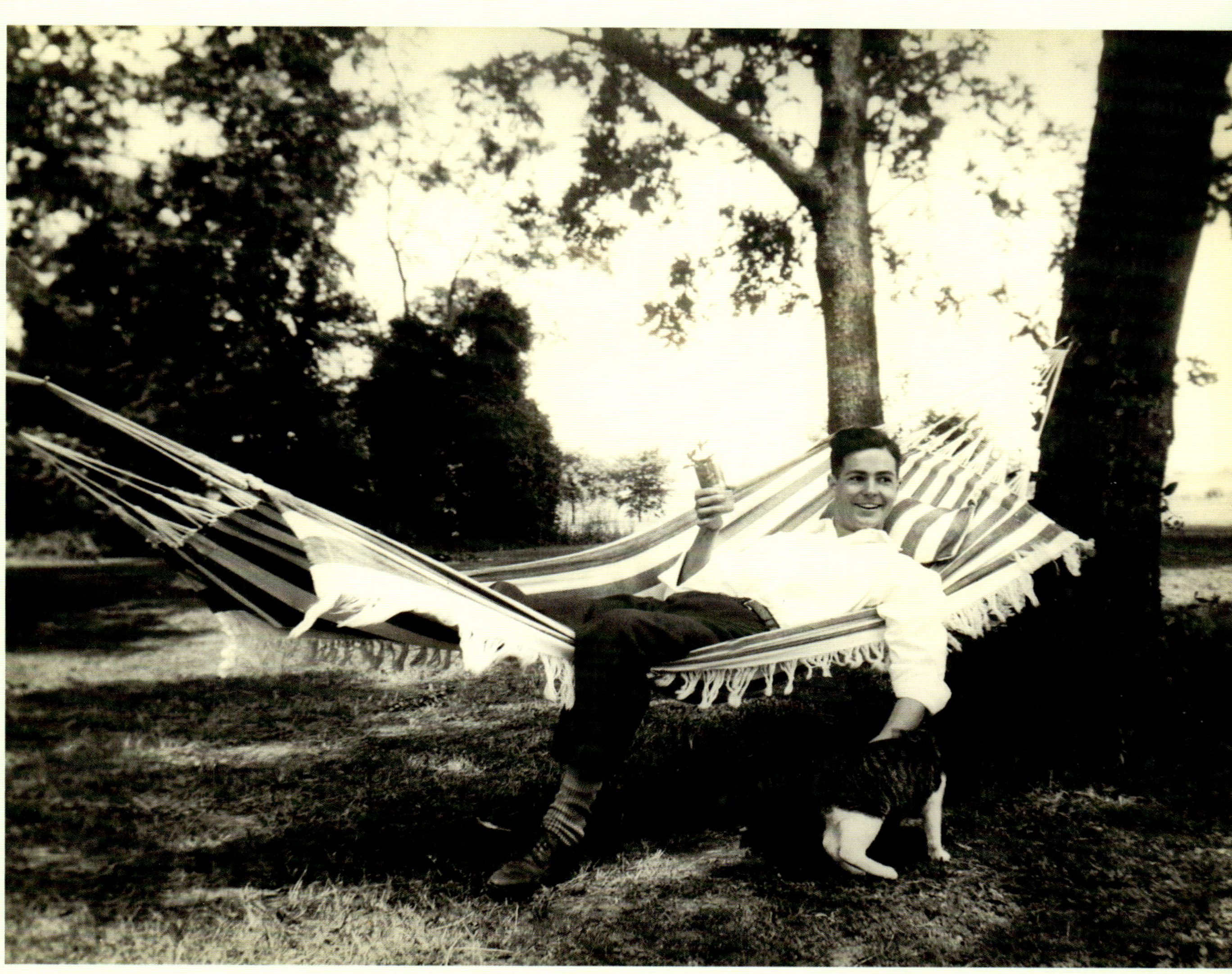

Photograph of the artist taken by his father, circa 1944.

Home is Where When You Go There, They Have to Take You In: The Life of Marshall Bouldin III

By Marshall Bouldin IV

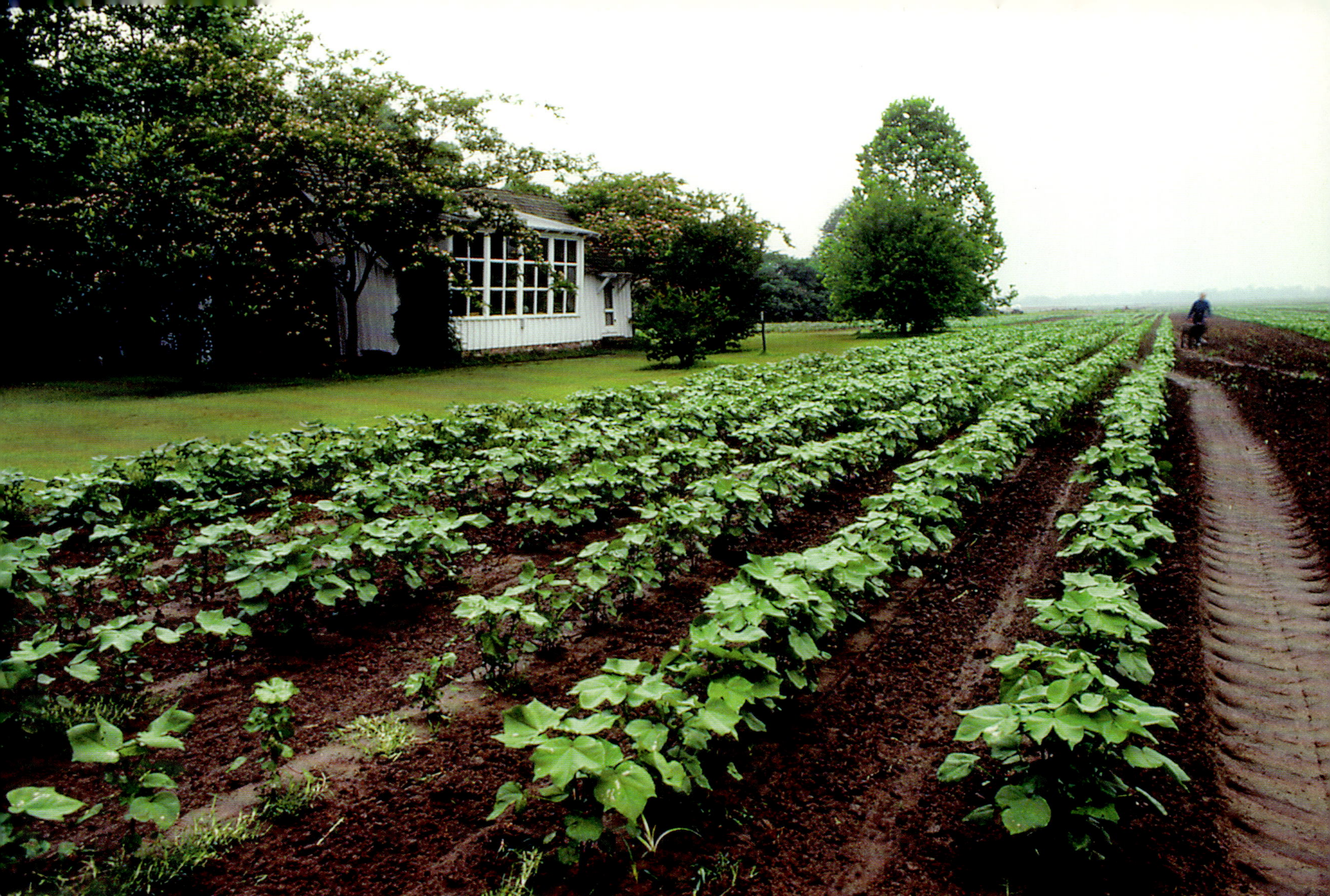

Strolling outside the studio, circa 1986.

Mississippi's artistic legacy is second to none in the United States. In every medium our artistic tradition is characterized by naturalness, practicality, honesty, and, ultimately, realism. These are the same qualities that distinguish the people of Mississippi. Our artistic legacy is so closely entwined with our daily lives here that we often overlook it. So it somehow seems unremarkable to us when we find in a Delta cotton field one of the foremost figures of American twentieth-century portraiture.

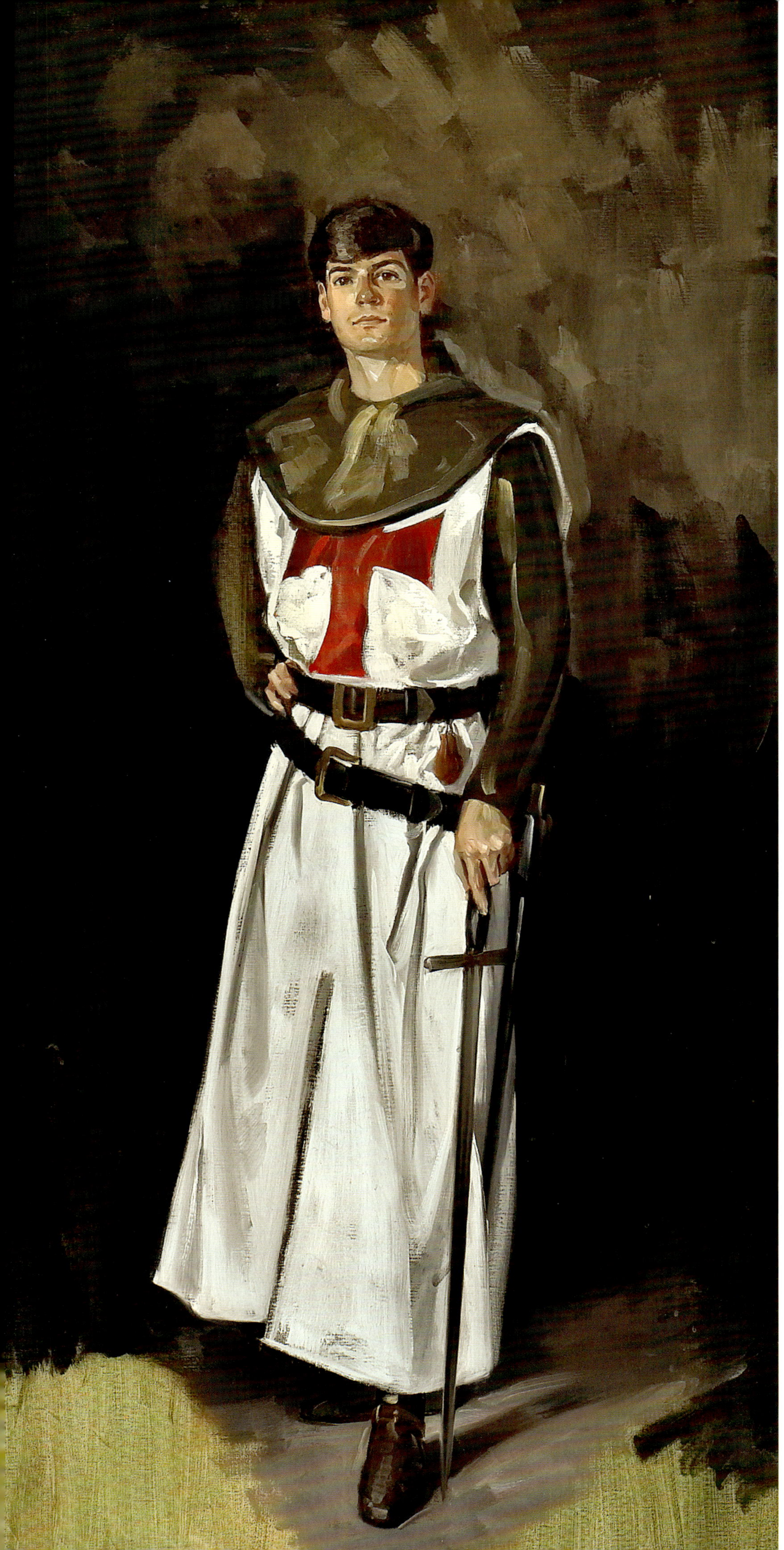

Portrait of Jason, circa 1986. oil on canvas. 84 x 42.

Having created over 800 professional portraits since he found his calling in 1956, Marshall Bouldin III is the elder statesman of American portraiture. Critics credit Bouldin with having an innate artistic gift. But Bouldin has always been quick to point to the true source of his success. "People say, 'Oh Mr. Bouldin, you're so talented. We just love your paintings.' And I've learned to say thank you. I know what they mean and that's wonderful, except that I know that they have missed the whole point. They are talking about artistic talent, as if it came down from above; but my talent isn't for that, whatever that may be. My talent is for discipline and work. Now, I'm standing there with my friend, who rents my land, who is the best farmer I've ever seen in my life. He's superior, but no one ever comes up to him and says what a talented farmer you are. And yet, his talent is just as much a talent as I have. But his real talent, his important talent, is the same as mine, which is just work."

Bouldin recalls an incident from his early days as an apprentice illustrator in New York in the 1940s. "After trying to be an artist for about a year, I went to two popular artists and asked for their advice. One was not very nice and looked at my work and told me to stick to the factory job I had. The other one, who worked for *Collier's* magazine, said, 'Marshall, you have a modicum of ability and if you expect to get anywhere, you're going to have to work hard.' At least he was on my side."

A Portrait of the Artist as a Young Man

Born on a breakfast room table in Dundee, Mississippi, in 1923, Bouldin suffered from a speech impediment and a partial paresis due to birth injuries. As a result, he couldn't keep up with his playmates and spent much of his childhood alone. This difference led him to express himself in drawing, and on his seventh birthday he received his first easel and paint set. Prior to Bouldin's graduation from high school in 1941, he won a scholarship to the Art Institute of Chicago. Up to that time, he had seen only a few original works of art, mostly in the Memphis Brooks Museum of Art. At the Art Institute, he came face-to-face with Van Gogh and impressionism for the first time. "I thought it was hogwash. I liked Rockwell. At that time, impressionism was beginning to fade and non-objective work was coming in. In a year and a half [at the Art Institute], they didn't teach me a thing. It was all, 'Be an artist; be yourself,' and just slop paint. I didn't know what the heck I was doing. I sloshed paint for a year and a half. I got so sick of it I quit.

"Still, it was the greatest time in my life for learning, because I was in the basement of the Art Institute, and every day I'd eat my lunch in fifteen minutes so I could go up and roam the galleries for forty-five minutes. I'd get out of school at four p.m. and the galleries closed at five p.m., so I'd just drink it in. I saw paintings I couldn't understand, but I kept looking and after that year and a half my tastes began to change."

To do his part for the war effort, Bouldin left the Institute and went to work in a Nashville aircraft factory, drawing blueprints for parts and indulging a budding love for illustration in his spare time. He met Norman Rockwell in 1946 and was inspired to apprentice himself to well-known magazine illustrators in Chicago, New York, and Westport, Connecticut. Magazine illustration was the order of the day, and Bouldin produced covers and illustrations for magazines such as *Outdoor Life*, *American Magazine*, and *Collier's*. But he was miserable.

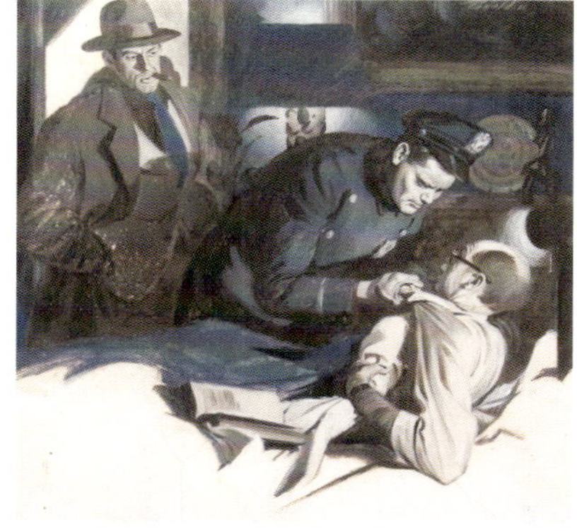

Come Clean, circa 1949. gouache on illustration board. 11 x 10½.

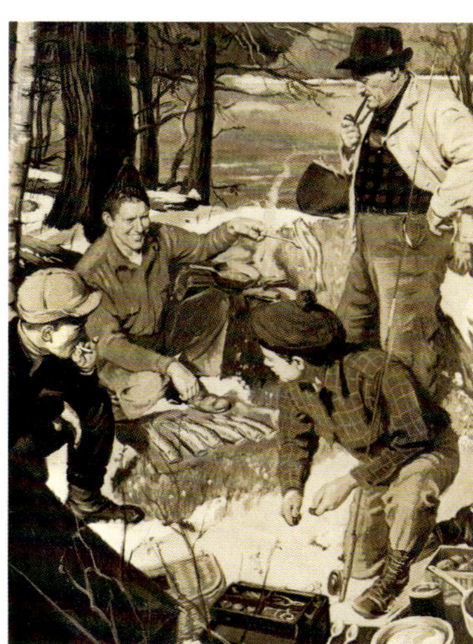

Illustration (originally in color) for Outdoor Life, *circa 1949.*

The turning point came three years later when he visited the Metropolitan Museum of Art in New York for a Van Gogh retrospective. "All of a sudden, boy, I saw a big Van Gogh, and I thought it was wonderful, beautiful, fantastic! I thought he was the greatest thing on earth. And before that I had thought he couldn't paint. Then I thought, 'My daddy has a farm. I can go home and farm and then I can just paint for fun.'"

. . . I will go home.

In 1950, Bouldin returned to his family farm and settled into a routine of farming during the week and painting on weekends. The next decade was for him a search for identity. He began with a period of painting "in the manner of" and progressed from Van Gogh to Renoir, Matisse, Picasso, and ultimately abstraction, eventually becoming bored and laying his paintbrush by. One day, he pulled out all of his paintings from the barn, hosed them off, and put them in the sun to dry. Looking at them all lined up, he realized that he had unconsciously followed the course of modern art from impressionism to the abstract present. "I didn't consciously follow the progression of modern art. I was trying to be an artist, and I was just having fun, just doing what I saw and what I liked."

Bouldin realized that all of his study and emulation had taught him to analyze a painting, which he saw as being made up of color, drawing, value, composition, and what he calls sentiment. He saw that the progression to modern art meant leaving out or radically modifying increasing numbers of these variables, leading to a departure from discipline and reality and, ultimately, through loss of constraint, to boredom. He needed a form of expression that returned those values.

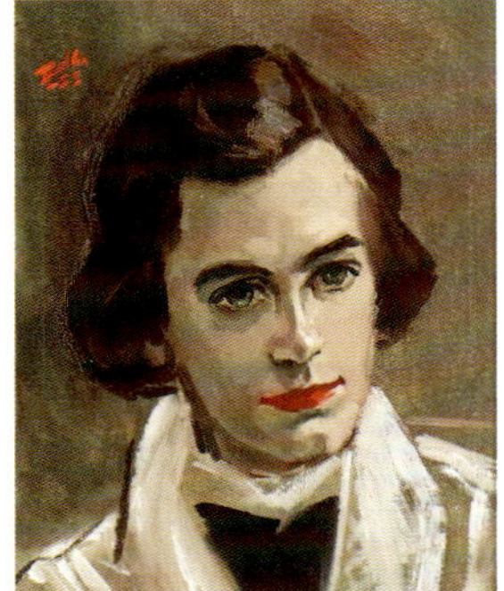

Mel, 1953. oil on canvas. 17 x 13.

"I realized then that the most memorable artists are the ones who may not be the best but they are the ones who start a trend. I thought to myself, if you can get to the next step, see the next step, you'll be the next great artist. So I said, 'O.K., what do you want to do? You started off wanting to be Norman Rockwell. You like to do people. And you like realism.' At the time, there was hardly anyone doing portraiture in the United States. It was all about modernism and the non-objective. I was still having fun, so I started to paint some farmhands. I'd pay them to sit for me. It was just for fun."

During this period, in 1954, he married his primary inspiration, his most important art critic, and the chief quality control agent of all his work, Mary Ellen Stribling. As Marshall did not quite fit farming, Mel did not quite fit the Delta housewife's life. So in about 1956, at a memorable family dinner, Marshall announced that he was quitting farming to make a living painting portraits, and Mel announced that she was going to medical school. The general consensus in Clarksdale was that they had lost their minds. Mel subsequently went on to become an accomplished obstetrician and gynecologist, flying her Cessna from the crop duster strip on the back of the place to her private practice in Memphis daily. She also served as Coahoma County's health officer for over thirty years. Marshall and Mel went on to have four sons: Marshall IV, Jamie, Mahlon, and Jason. Bouldin's family has always been the center of his life. As he says with a laugh, "Historically, you know, debt has always been the motivation behind great art."

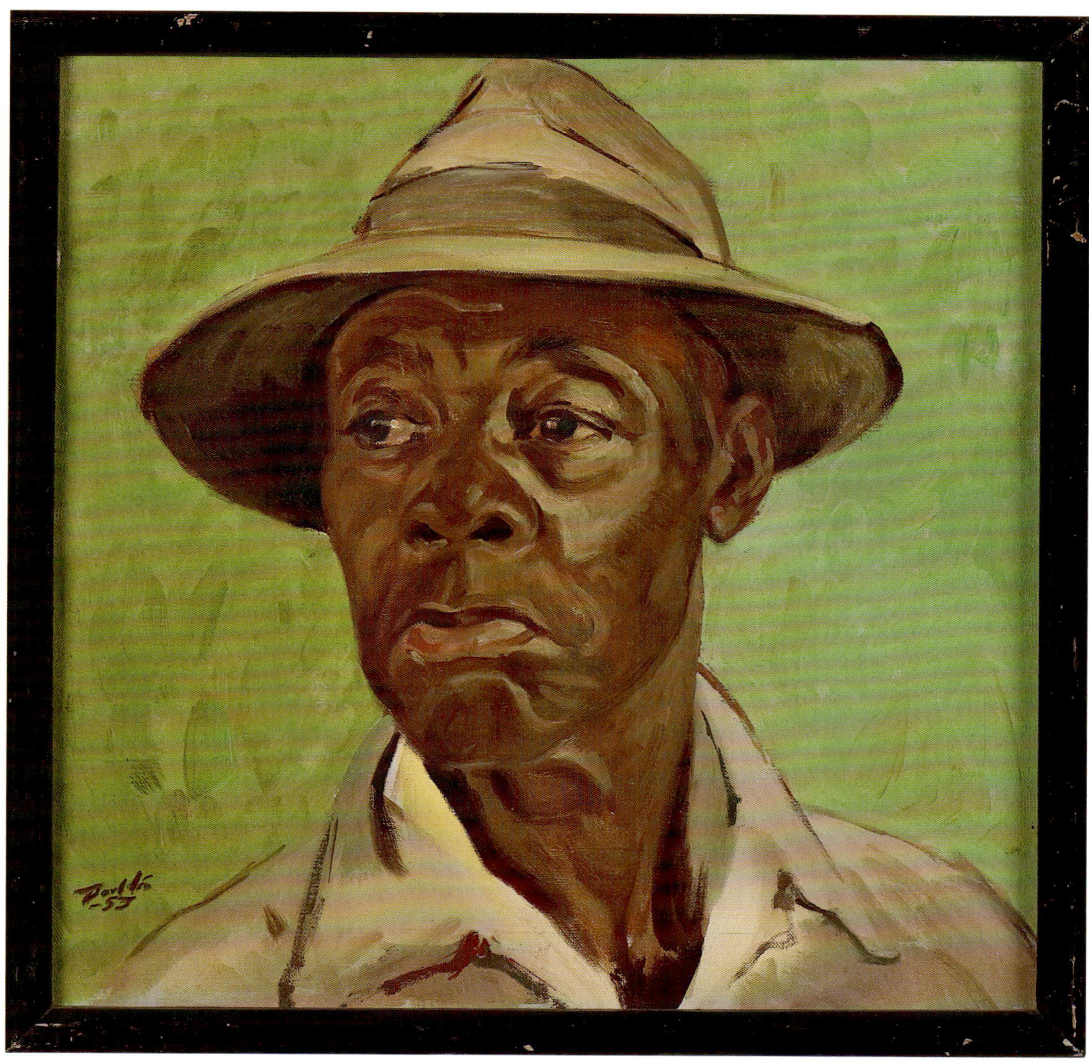

John Brown, 1953. oil on canvas. 16 x 16.

The Hundred Dollars

Bouldin's first portrait, of field hand John Brown (1953), sits today in Bouldin's studio alongside his first "real" portrait, a copy of a Henry Raeburn that hangs in the Memphis Brooks Museum of Art. It took two years and some financial necessity to get from the one to the other. A family friend had tried repeatedly to hire Bouldin to paint a portrait, and Bouldin kept refusing because he felt that technically he wasn't ready. Bouldin explains, "Finally [my friend] said to me, 'Well, I've got $100.' I said, 'What?!' I said, 'I can't paint it now, but I'll tell you what. You hang on to that $100. I'm going to get that $100.'"

So he began to study. His wife had brought home a box of bones from medical school, and in playing with the skull, Bouldin was intrigued at how much it was really like a brickbat. He remembered all that he had learned about the perspective drawing of brickbats and similar mechanical objects back at the aircraft factory. So he spent the next nine months drawing and studying anatomy,

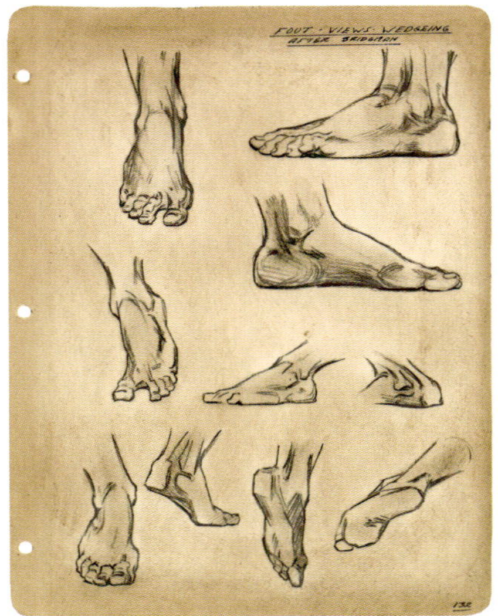

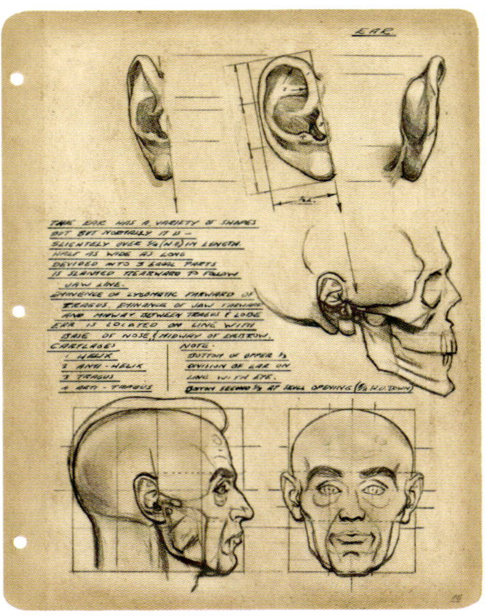

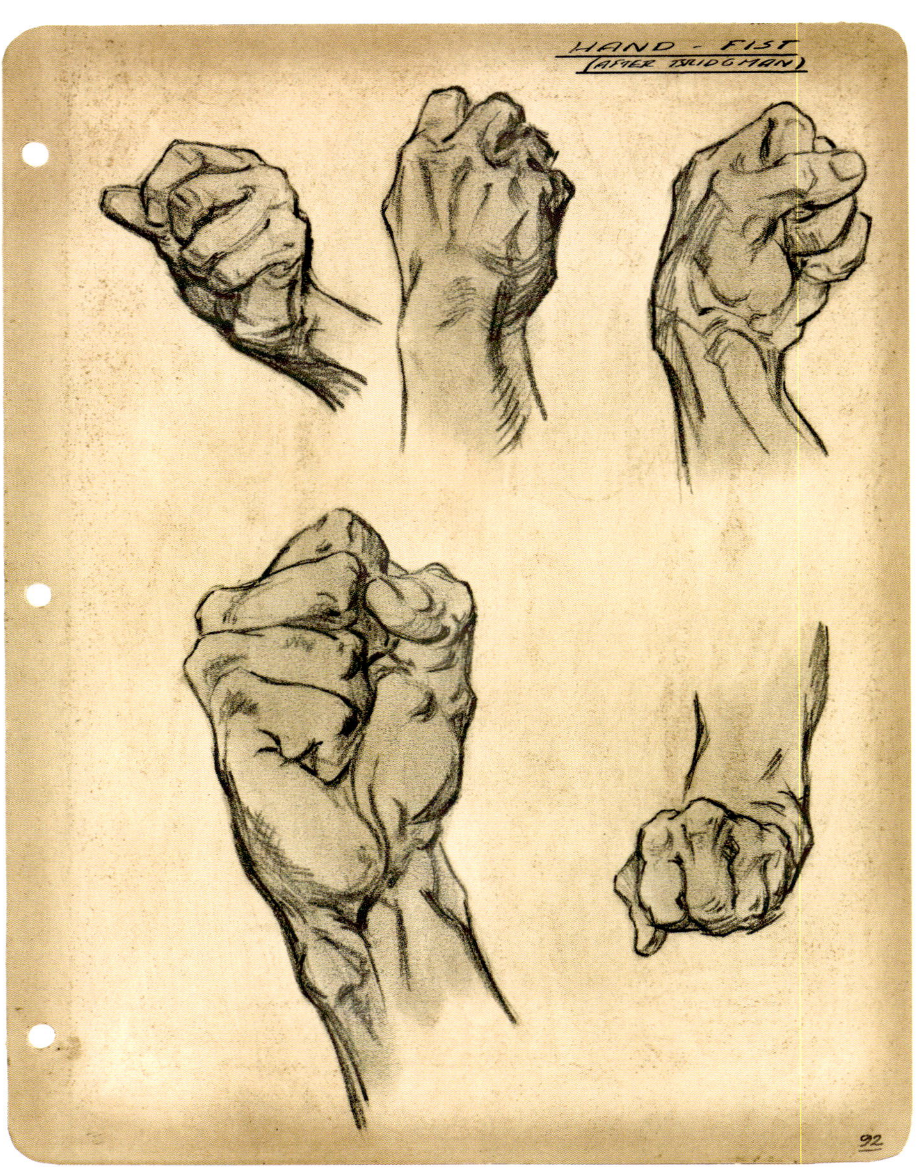

Foot – Views – Wedgeing (after Bridgman), page 132; **Ear**, page 16; **Hand – Fist (after Bridgman)**, page 92; from anatomy book, circa 1956–1958, graphite and ink on paper, 11 x 8½, each.

making a book that his son, Jason, also a portrait artist, keeps and uses to this day. From there, he went on to color and spent the next two years studying the color wheel and learning to mix and match color. When his wife chided him for this seemingly perpetual course of study, he set himself a "thesis," which was to copy that Raeburn in the Brooks museum.

So, two years later, in 1958, Bouldin went back to his friend. "I said, 'Do you still have that $100, because I want it.'" The commission, ironically, was to paint Bouldin's late grandfather, Marshall Bouldin, who had been his friend's former boss at Delta Grocery and Cotton Company. "He gave me the $100, and when I was delivering the portrait, Mr. Max Ladt was standing there and asked, 'Can you paint my portrait?' So I said, 'You got $100?' When I delivered Mr. Ladt's there were four more people standing in line. That first fall, I made $600. So I told my daddy, 'I can't farm anymore. This is too good to be true.' And that's how I got started."

I am a part of all that I have known…

Thus began Bouldin's fifty-two-year career in portraiture, a career characterized by quiet, continuous, voluminous production and a constant striving to better the last portrait. Highlights from that career include portraits for then president Richard Nixon of his two daughters, official portraits for many national political figures, including Thad Cochran, Sam Ervin, Claude Pepper, Tom Foley, Jack Brooks, Jamie Whitten, John Stennis, James Eastland, Jim Wright, many Mississippi governors, William Faulkner, and astronaut Ron McNair, among others. Bouldin painted many private commissions across the country for distinguished leaders of industry, business, agriculture, academics, and the church. He has also exhibited at the Royal Portrait Society exhibition in London.

Perhaps his most fulfilling commission was the private portrait of Nathan Cummings, CEO of General Foods/Sarah Lee and a world-renowned fine art collector. "For the portrait, I had to copy a Monet which I had always admired, because it was part of the background, hanging right over the desk. He took a Gauguin down to hang my portrait. A large Picasso was on the wall opposite. There was even a Degas in the bathroom."

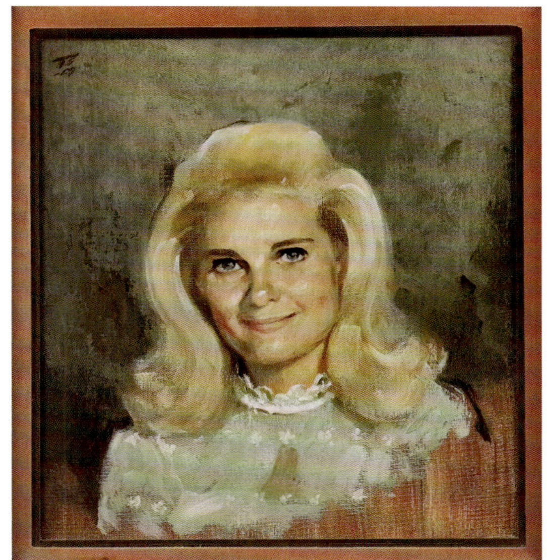

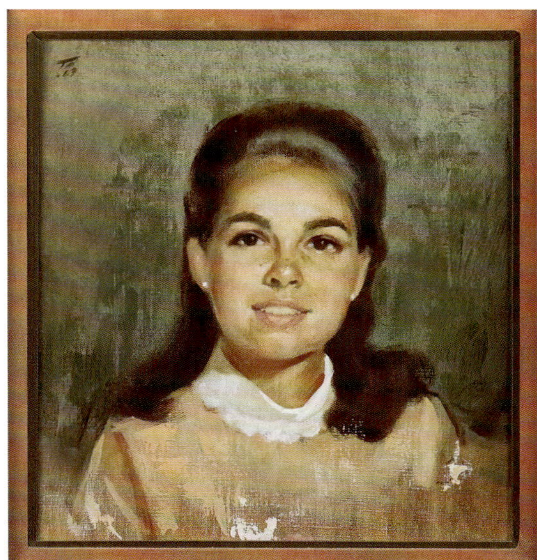

Preliminary Study for Tricia Nixon, 1969. oil on canvas. 13 x 12. **Preliminary Study for Julie N. Eisenhower**, 1969. oil on canvas. 13 x 12.

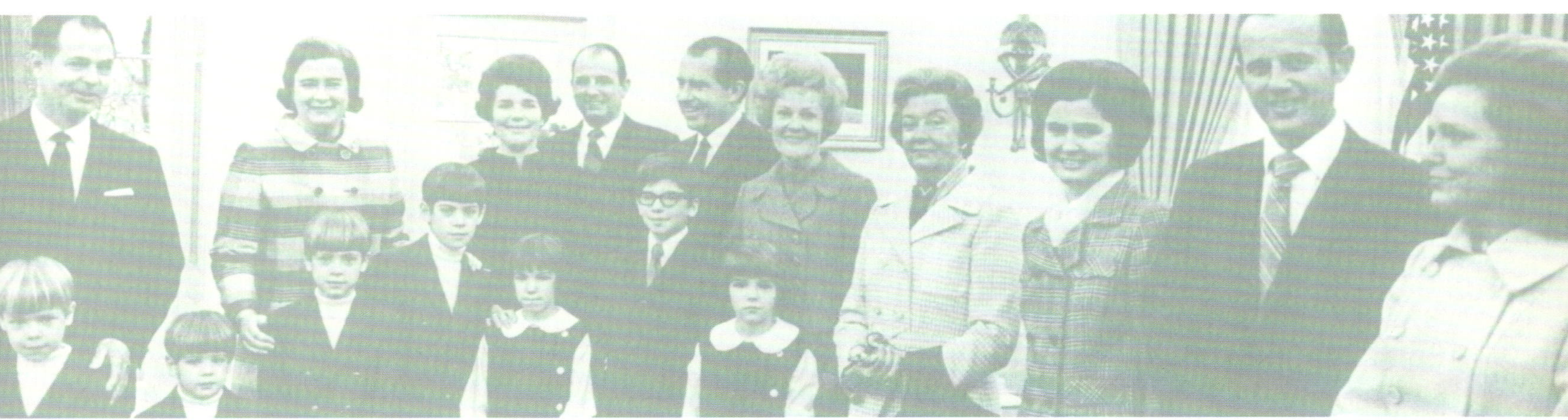

The Bouldin family and guests present President and Mrs. Nixon with Bouldin's portrait of their daughters, Julie and Tricia.

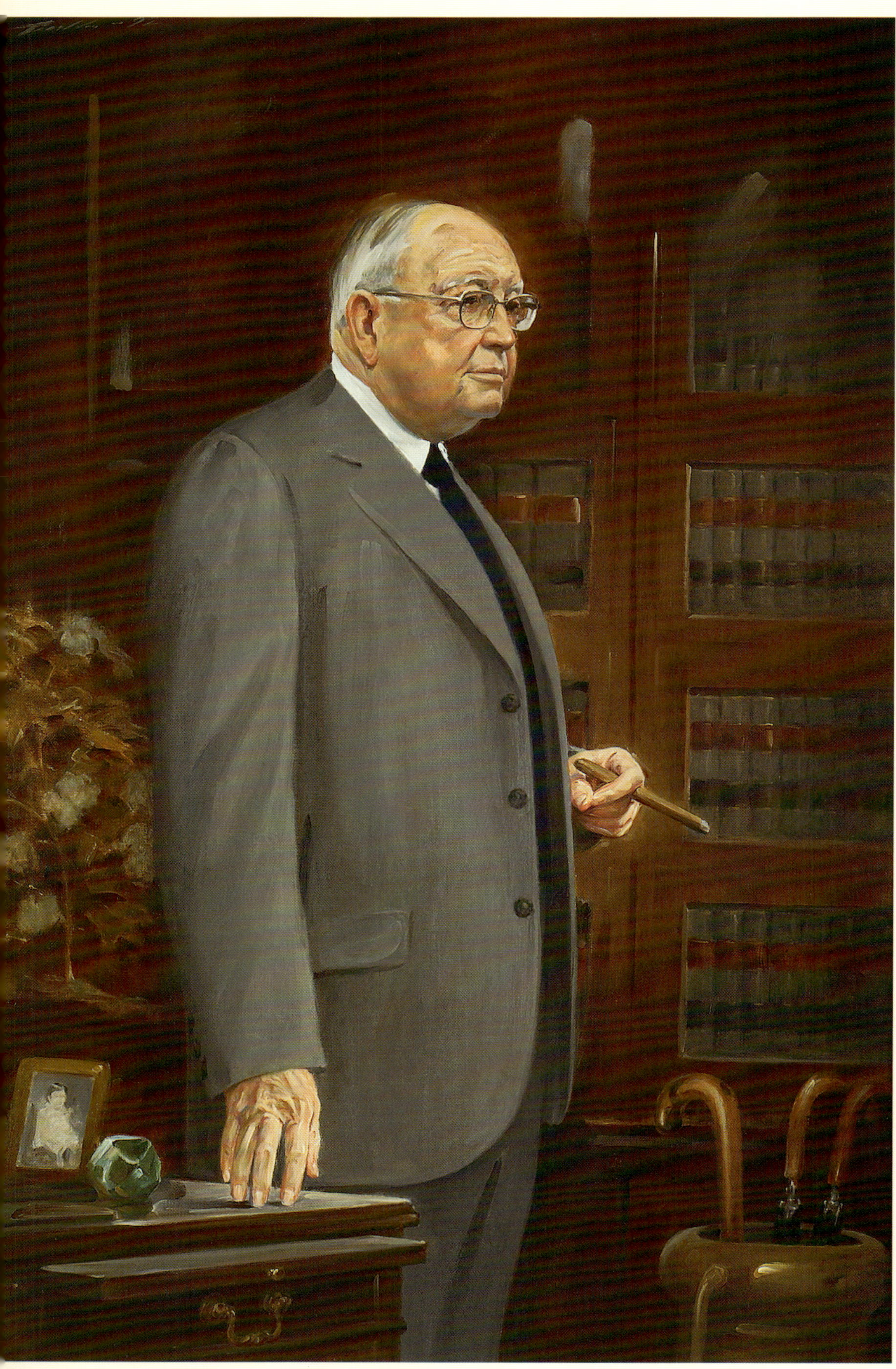

Senator James Eastland, 1992. oil on canvas. $52\frac{1}{4}$ x $34\frac{1}{2}$. *Collection of the Museum of Mississippi History, Mississippi Department of Archives and History, Jackson. 1992.22.1.*

In addition to life sketches, Bouldin's self-developed method incorporates personal interviews, color sketches, photographs, and videos of his subjects, ideally in their home environment. He watches their movements and studies their expressions, their postures, and their mannerisms until he understands their feeling, their essential presence. He often takes hundreds of photographs before a subject stops self-consciously posing and lets his or her true self come out.

"You've got to know the person first, because there's a difference between a portrait of a person and a picture of a person. People don't really look at you. They know who you are and recognize you, but they really don't look at you. People go on your personality. They feel you, just like an animal does. People emanate feelings, which other people pick up. And this feeling is the main thing that goes into a real portrait."

Now eighty-five, Bouldin has said he will work until he is 101 and then quit "whether or not I have made the grade." His schedule for fifty years has been true to his major talent—work. He rises at five a.m. every day and paints straight through to six p.m. He does take Sunday mornings off to attend church but is back in the studio in the afternoon. "I work so much because I simply enjoy it. I don't always love my work, but I love working."

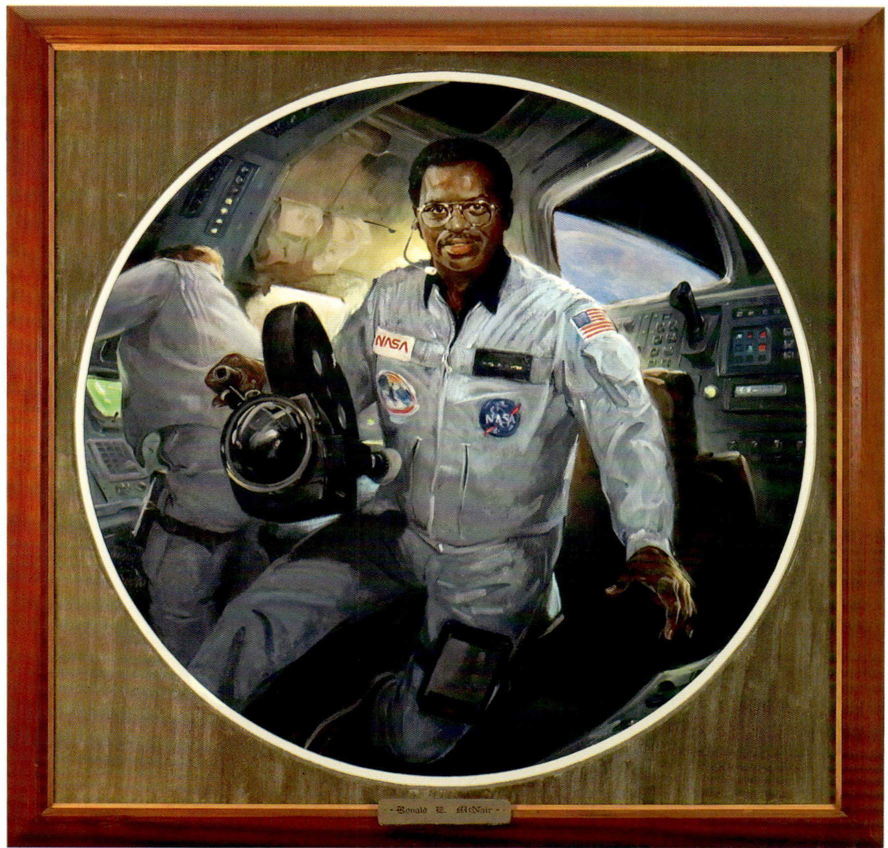

Ronald E. McNair, 1986. oil on canvas. 54½ x 54½. *Collection of Russell C. Davis Planetarium, Jackson, Mississippi.*

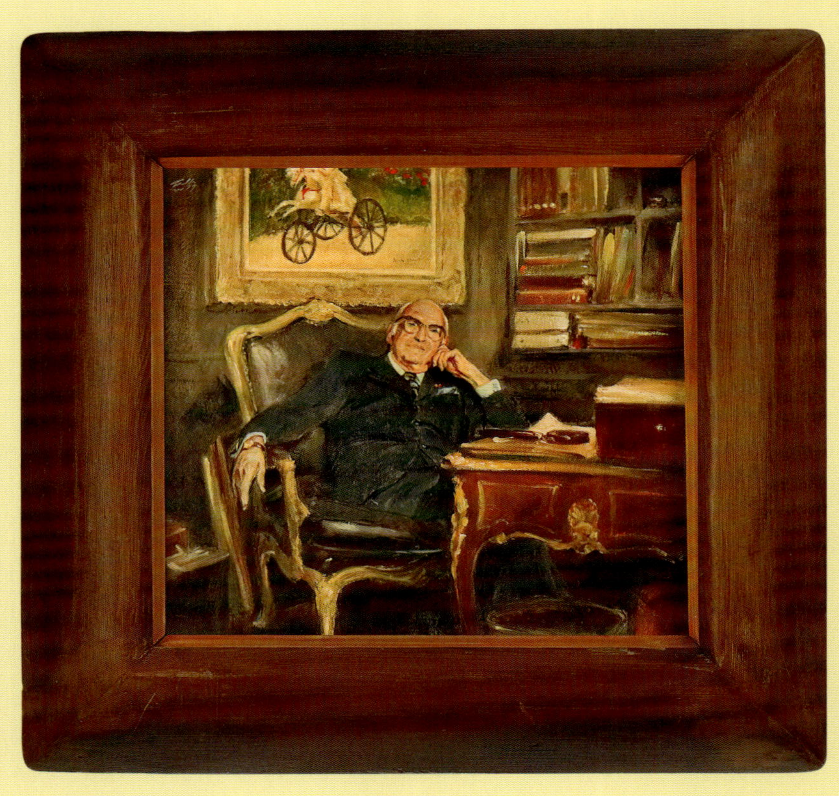

Preliminary Study for Nathan Cummings, 1977. oil on canvas. 14 x 16.

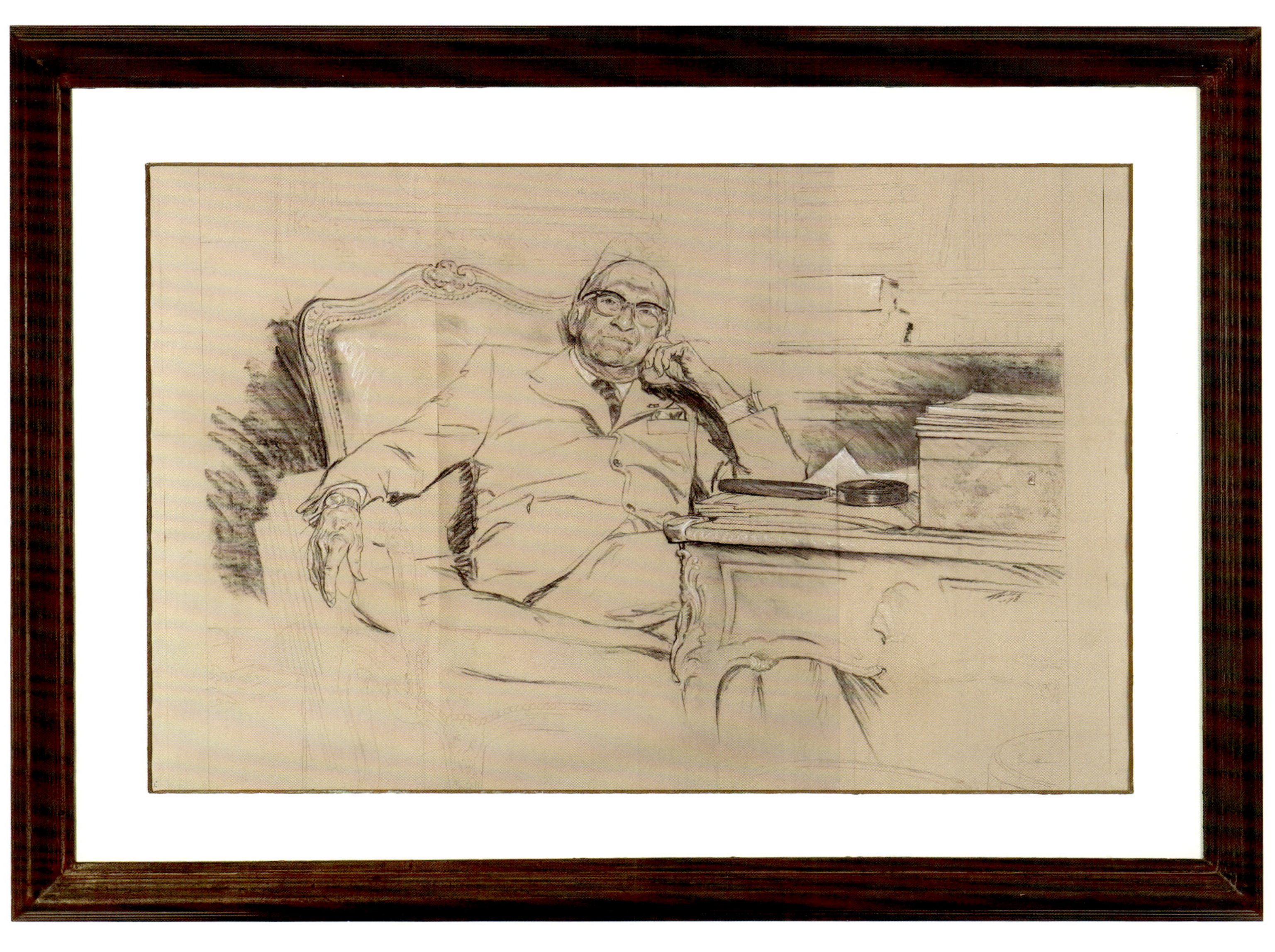

Preliminary Study for Nathan Cummings, 1978. charcoal on paper. 31 x 46 (sight).

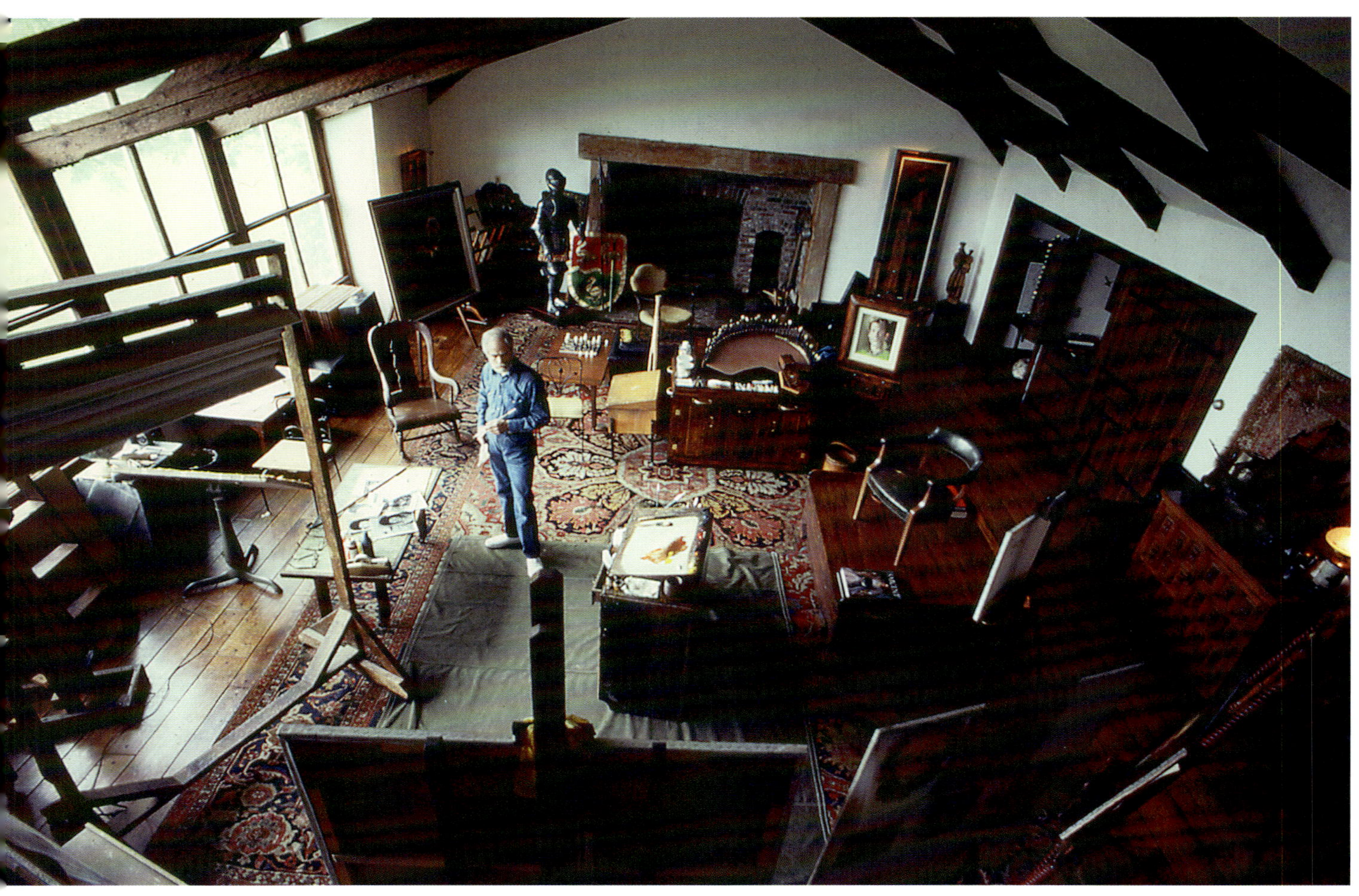

At work in studio, circa 1986.

Lessons of a life

The life of Marshall Bouldin III gives us a window to see in ourselves what we as Mississippians so often take for granted. We see that, even if you never leave a Delta cotton field, through introspection, drive, and hard work you can realize your dreams and achieve national recognition and leadership in your field. We see that work, rather than genius, talent, or advantage, is indeed primary. And we see and feel that God has a plan for and a place in our lives and in those around us.

Bouldin feels he has been called by God to be a portrait artist. "I feel so close to God, so related to God. I have a call to be a portrait painter, to paint the best portrait possible, regardless of the money. And if I don't, I'm cheating myself, and cheating everybody else. It's all so beautiful; and I get to do what I want!"

A Painter's Odyssey

The Art of Marshall Bouldin III

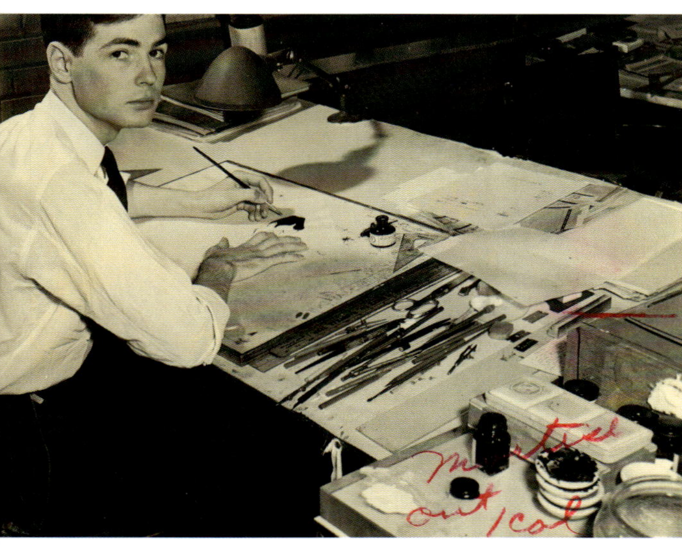

Drawing caricatures of employees at aircraft factory, Nashville, Tennessee, circa 1943–1945.

Over the course of a professional career that has spanned more than fifty years, Marshall Bouldin III has earned international recognition for his remarkable accomplishments as a portrait painter. The sitters for his more than 800 portraits have been diverse, ranging from CEOs to congressmen, generals to astronauts, symphony conductors to literary figures, as well as ordinary men, women, and children. A member of the American Society of Portrait Artists, Bouldin has also exhibited with the Royal Society of British Artists in London, and his works are included in numerous private, corporate, and public collections. Though he is best known for his commission portraiture, it constitutes but one aspect of the painter's vast and varied output. The story of the artistic paths he has traveled over the decades is fascinating and illuminating.

Born in Dundee, Mississippi, in 1923, Bouldin suffered from congenital physical problems that prevented him from participating in many childhood activities. Introspective by nature, he found solace and inspiration in drawing, was recognized by classmates and teachers for his skillful creations, and continued his artwork throughout his teens. Like so many budding artists of his generation, Bouldin was influenced by the work of Norman Rockwell (1894-1978) and other illustrators whose images he saw in popular magazines. In 1941, with a scholarship awarded him by *Scholastic Magazine*, Bouldin entered the School of the Art Institute of Chicago, intending to pursue a career as an illustrator. During his free hours outside the classroom, he wandered through the nearby galleries of the Institute and immersed himself in the myriad masterworks he found there. While Bouldin responded enthusiastically to the older realistic or naturalistic canvases, he was often puzzled by some of the recent, more avant-garde images. The solitary, contemplative time he spent in the galleries would ultimately prove to be an integral part of his artistic development.

In April 1942, discouraged by what he felt was the lack of constructive, formal classroom training, Bouldin left the school. Physically unable to serve in the military, he contributed to the war effort by translating blueprints into isometric assembly plans for the workers in a Nashville aircraft factory. Following the war, he embarked upon his long-anticipated career as an illustrator, apprenticing at studios in Chicago and Westport, Connecticut. After several years, however, Bouldin found the practice of illustration unrewarding and at odds with his own creative hunger. He returned to Clarksdale in 1950 to help his father manage the family cotton plantation. After each day on the job, he painted for himself.

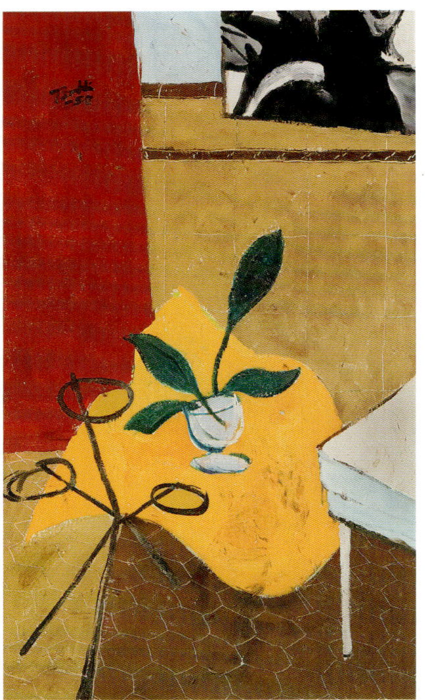

Still Life, 1953. oil on canvas. 44 x 26.

Seeking a Voice

If the creative confinement of illustration had frustrated Bouldin, the new freedom to paint without limitation was initially confounding. He struggled to find his own aesthetic voice by exploring the work of others, and in 1950 he began to paint in series inspired by masters he recalled from his wanderings in the Art Institute galleries. Armed with his brush, imagination, and resolve, he worked prodigiously in this manner, progressing from true-to-nature to truly abstract compositions.

The series work proved to be invaluable to Bouldin's artistic growth. Through this practice he came to understand aesthetic concepts that previously had been foreign to him, expanded the range of his technical mastery, and broadened his knowledge of art history. For example, inspired by Vincent van Gogh's (1853-1890) memorable images of French peasants at work in the fields, Bouldin depicted Mississippi tenant farmers gathering hay with rich hues and thick, impasto surfaces; he rendered a local piano teacher with flickering brushwork evoking the impressionist Pierre Renoir (1841-1919); and he painted an interior in broad, flat areas of vivid color recalling the bold pictorial simplification of Henri Matisse (1869-1954). In 1954, Bouldin abandoned the series work and committed himself to painting in a realist manner.

Bouldin began to paint subjects close at hand, hoping to develop a reputation as a regionalist and find a market for his work.The greater visual vocabulary and enhanced technical skills he had developed through the

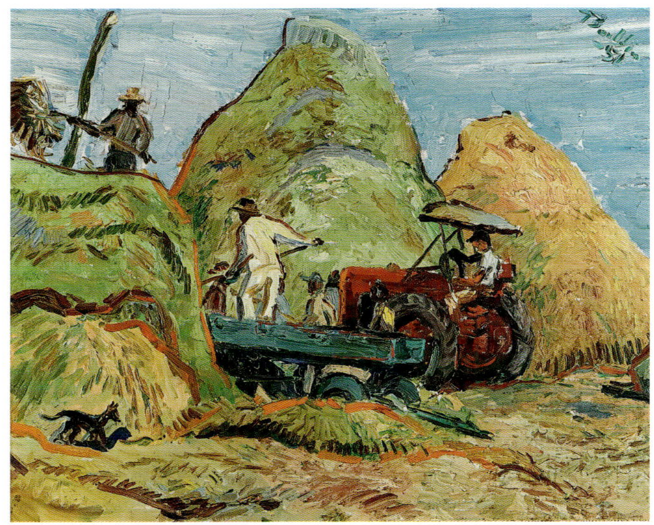

Stacking Hay, 1951. oil on canvas. 26 x 32.

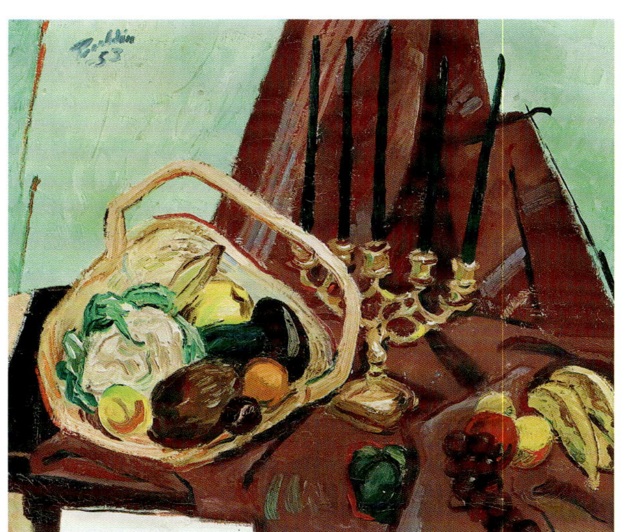

Still Life, 1953. oil on canvas. 26 x 30.

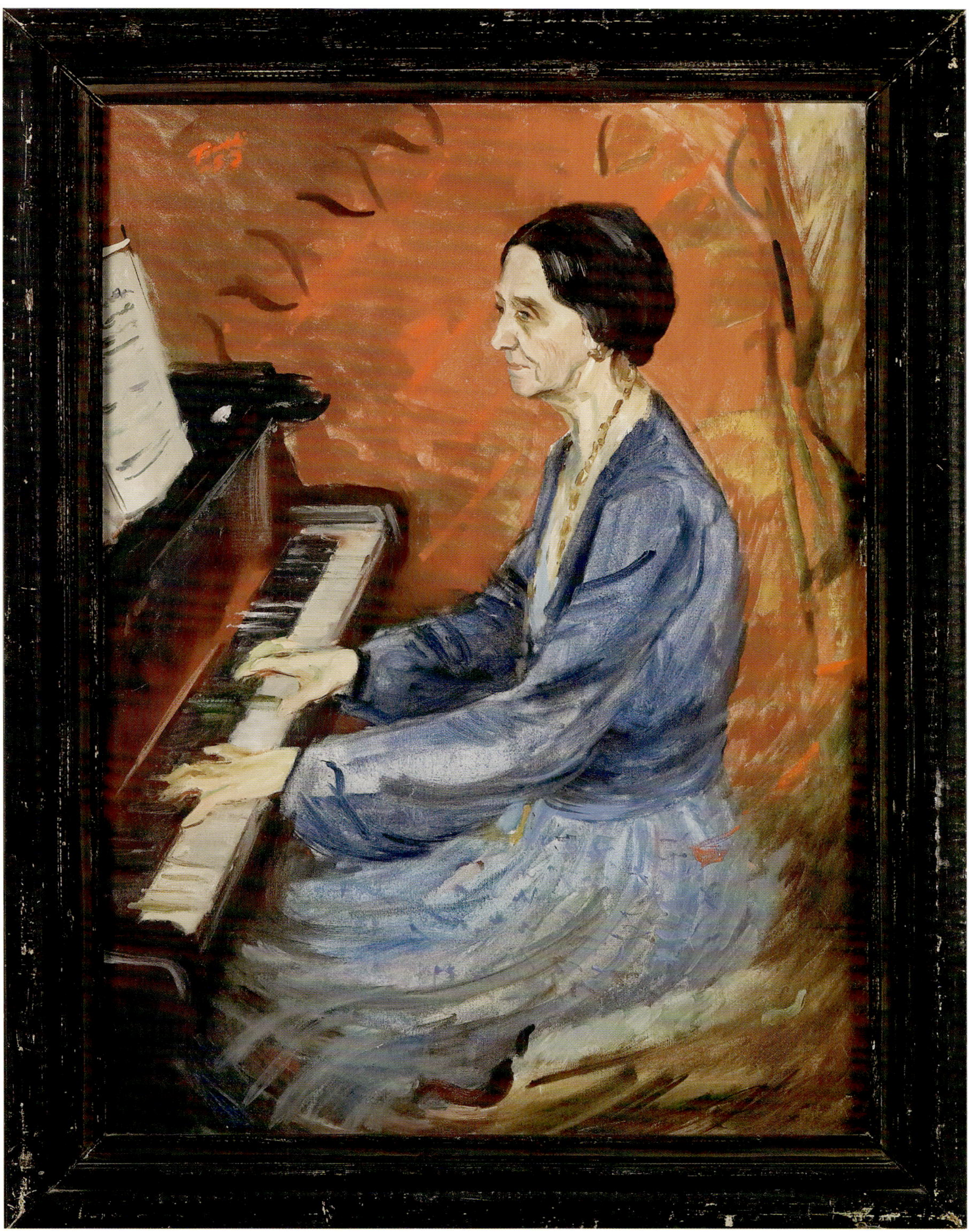

Miss Ada Chapman, 1953. oil on canvas. 36 x 26.

series works were evident in the new paintings, as was his abiding love for his state and compassion for its people. The artist's searching eye found the beauty of its changing landscape vistas, from the banks of the Mississippi River to the verdant Delta. He also depicted Mississippians at work, and some who struggled against difficult circumstances. *Second Notice*, circa 1954, is a solemn and compelling reminder of the hardscrabble existence led by sharecroppers. Bouldin's sophisticated pictorial structure and vigorously brushed palette of muted grays, greens, and browns lend this modest-scale canvas considerable emotional impact. A grim narrative plays out across the spacious landscape, as the viewer's eye moves rhythmically across the mule, man, woman, and the ominous white note.

While Bouldin was primarily focused on landscape and genre paintings during the early 1950s, he also began to paint small, informal portraits for his own satisfaction, with no thought of selling them. These works demonstrate his budding interest in and innate gift for portraiture, as well as his ability to empathize with sitters. In *Mel*, 1953, a portrait of the woman he would wed, the artist captures his subject's intelligence, determination, and beauty, and betrays his fascination with her. The painting's somber palette is enlivened by his loose, nervous brush strokes, and punctuated by her large dark eyes and bright red lips.

The frequent subjects of the early portraits were the African American working men and women with whom he interacted daily on the family plantation. By presenting the sitters in their everyday clothes and set against a spare background, Bouldin focuses the viewer's attention on their faces. He masterfully captures each distinctive mien, evincing not only his keen powers of observation but also his emotional connection to the subject. Bouldin defines each as an individual, with inner strength and human dignity.

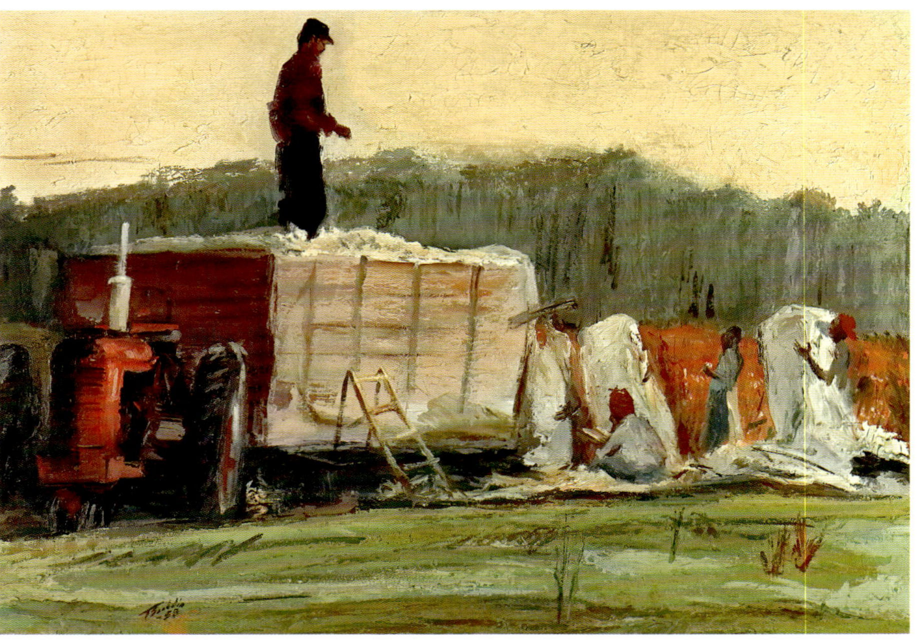

Lewis Stompin' Cotton, 1958. oil on canvas. 28 x 48.

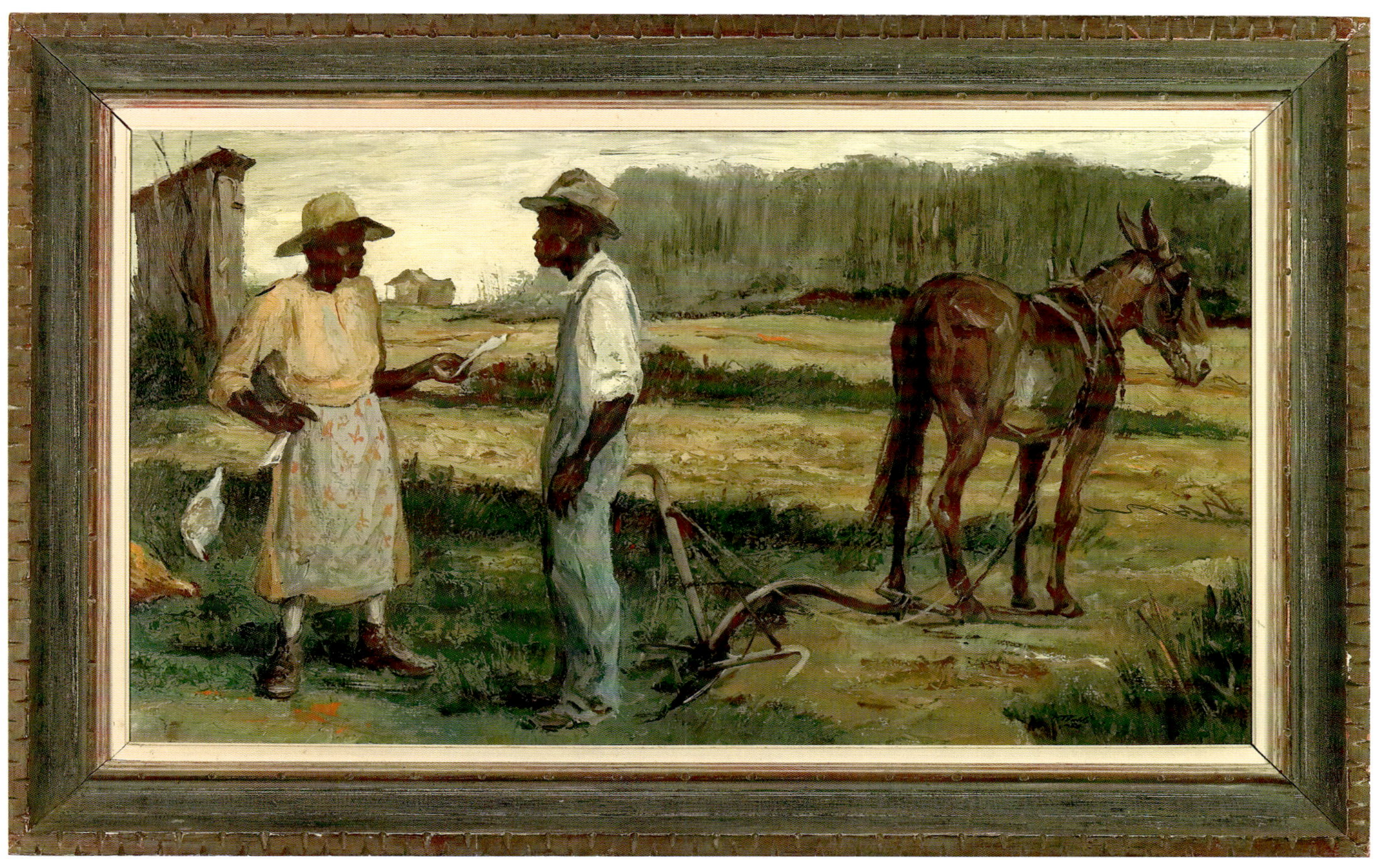

Second Notice, circa 1954. oil on canvas. 24 x 42.

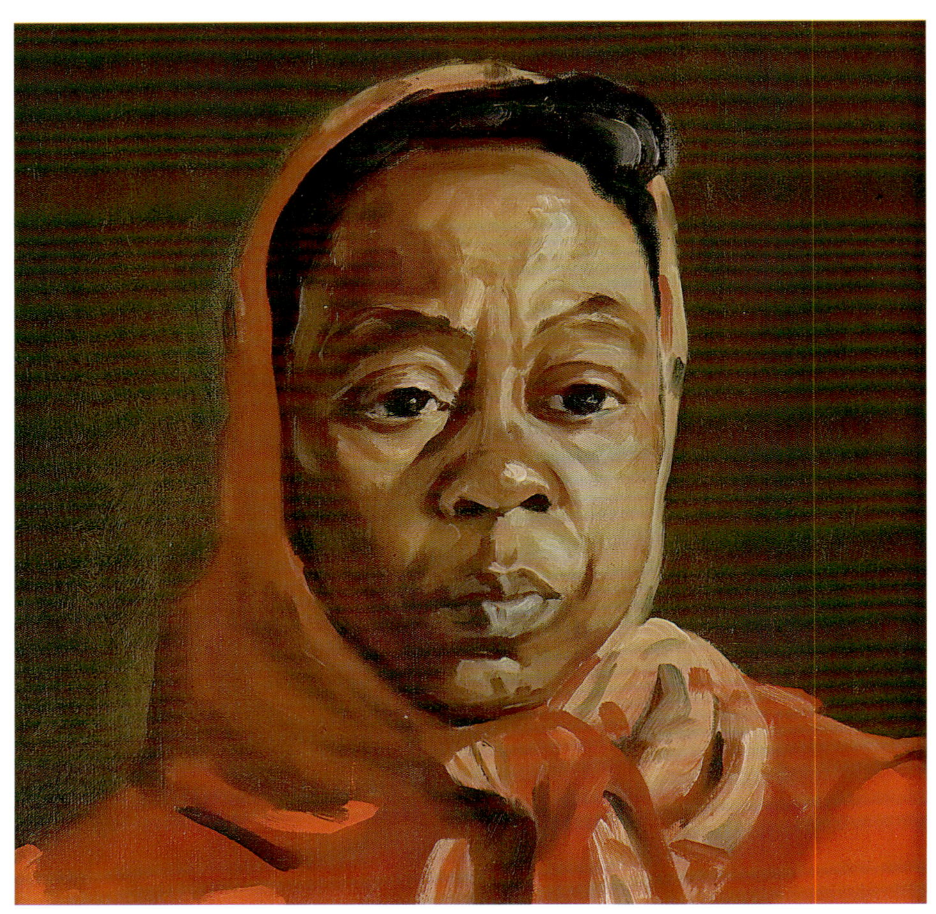

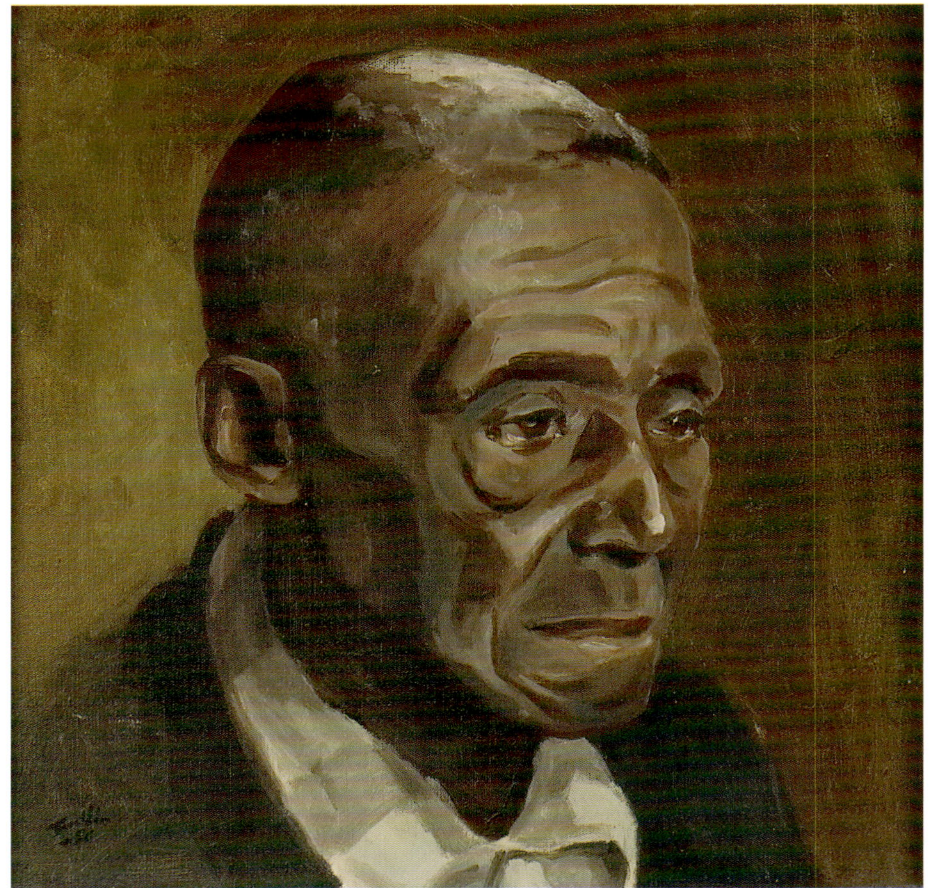

Aunt Bea, 1956. oil on canvas. 16 x 16.

Sam Webb, 1956. oil on canvas. 16 x 16.

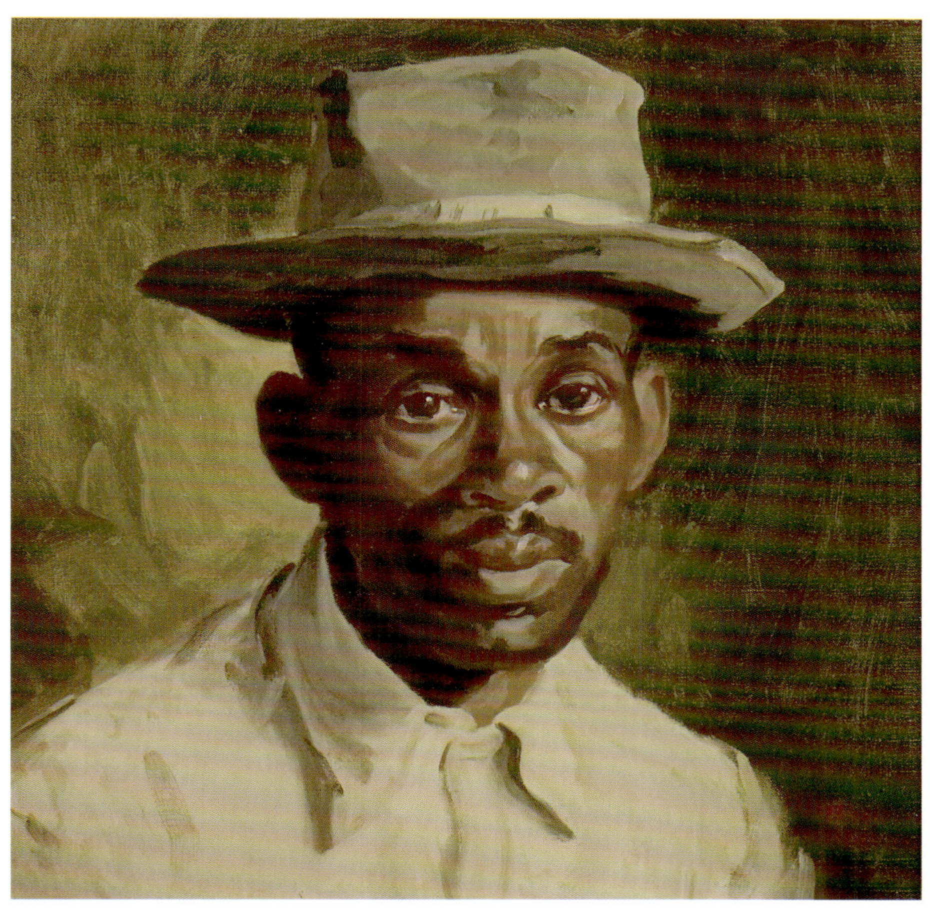

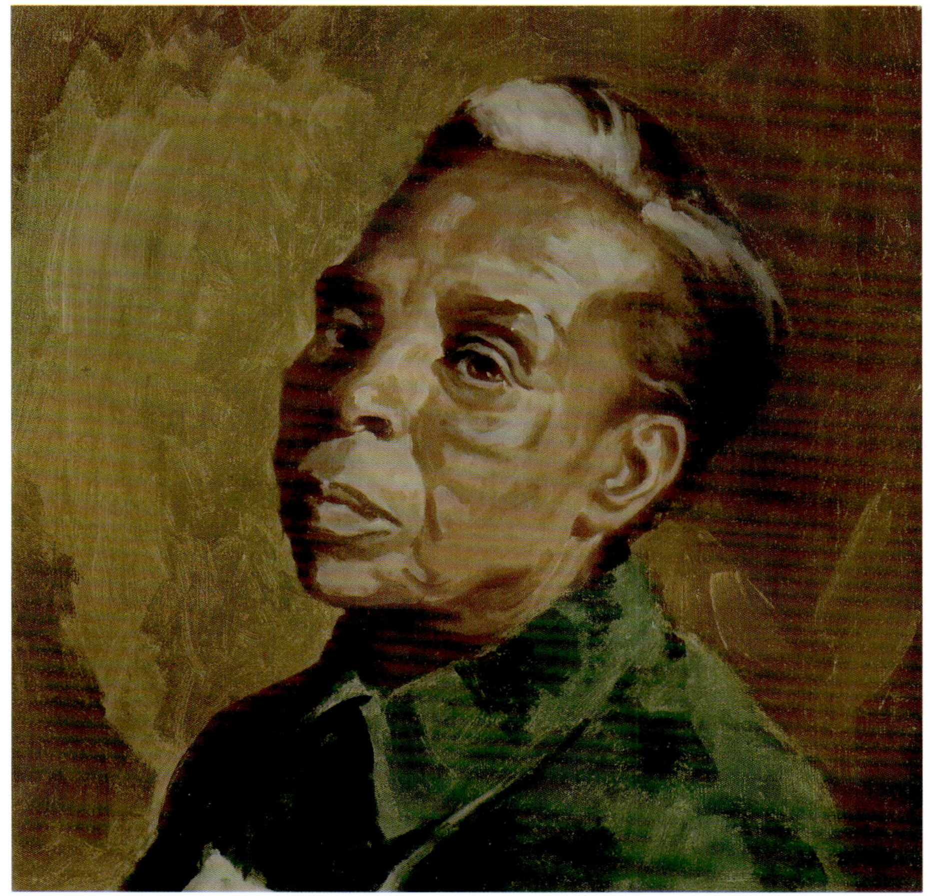

Charlie Miller, 1956. oil on canvas. 16 x 16.

They Endured (Cordelia Monagham), 1956. oil on canvas. 16 x 16.

One painter will always turn his model into a still life...[and]...create an inanimate object, without thought or speech....But [another] painter wants the illusion of giving life to life, he feels the need to rise to a more spiritual level than if he were merely molding a vase.[1]

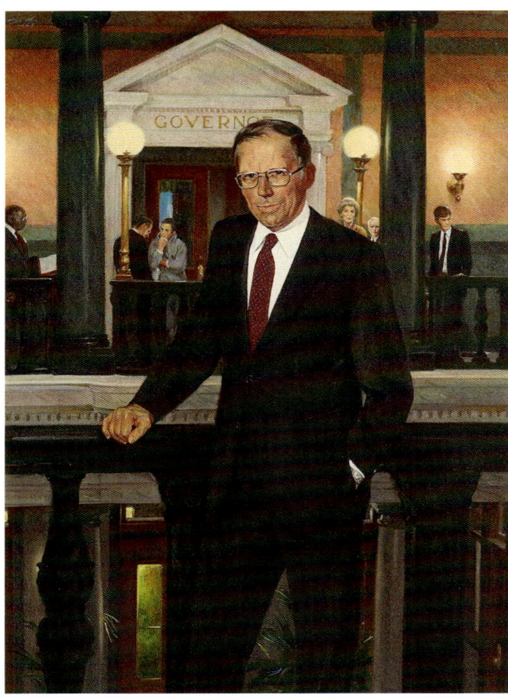

Governor William Winter, 1983. oil on canvas. $47\frac{1}{4}$ x $34\frac{1}{4}$. *Collection of the Museum of Mississippi History, Mississippi Department of Archives and History, Jackson. 1983.49.1.*

The Portraitist

By 1956 Bouldin had yet to establish a steady clientele for his regionalist art, despite his tireless efforts. One day a visitor to his studio, admiring one of the portraits of a sharecropper, suggested that Bouldin could establish a career as a commission portraitist if he showed examples of his work to people of means. Hopeful but not yet convinced, Bouldin ventured forth with samples, and soon found a willing client in a local merchant. Having won his first commission, Bouldin asked that it be delayed while he polished his skills as a portraitist.

Intent on schooling himself, he drew the figure prolifically from life, created his own anatomy book, painstakingly mixed and cataloged for reference some 4,500 color samples, and refined his oil painting techniques.[2] He developed his own portrait procedure, customarily beginning with figure and composition studies in graphite or charcoal, following with oil color sketches, and then advancing to the final painting on canvas. To prove to himself that he was ready for portraiture, he called once again upon the masters and painted exacting copies of canvases by William Merritt Chase (1849-1916), Diego Velasquez (1599-1660), John Singer Sargent (1856-1925), and others.

In 1958, after two years of tireless preparation, he returned to the waiting client and launched his career as a professional commission portraitist. At the outset, his usual subjects were local men or their wives or children. But as the artist's reputation grew, the sitters increasingly hailed from greater distances, and came to include prominent figures. Since the 1968 portrait of Julie and Tricia Nixon that first gave him national exposure, his sitters have included such notables as Speaker of the House of Representatives Jim Wright, Senator John Stennis, Governor William Winter, astronaut Ronald E. McNair, General Louis Wilson, and author William Faulkner.

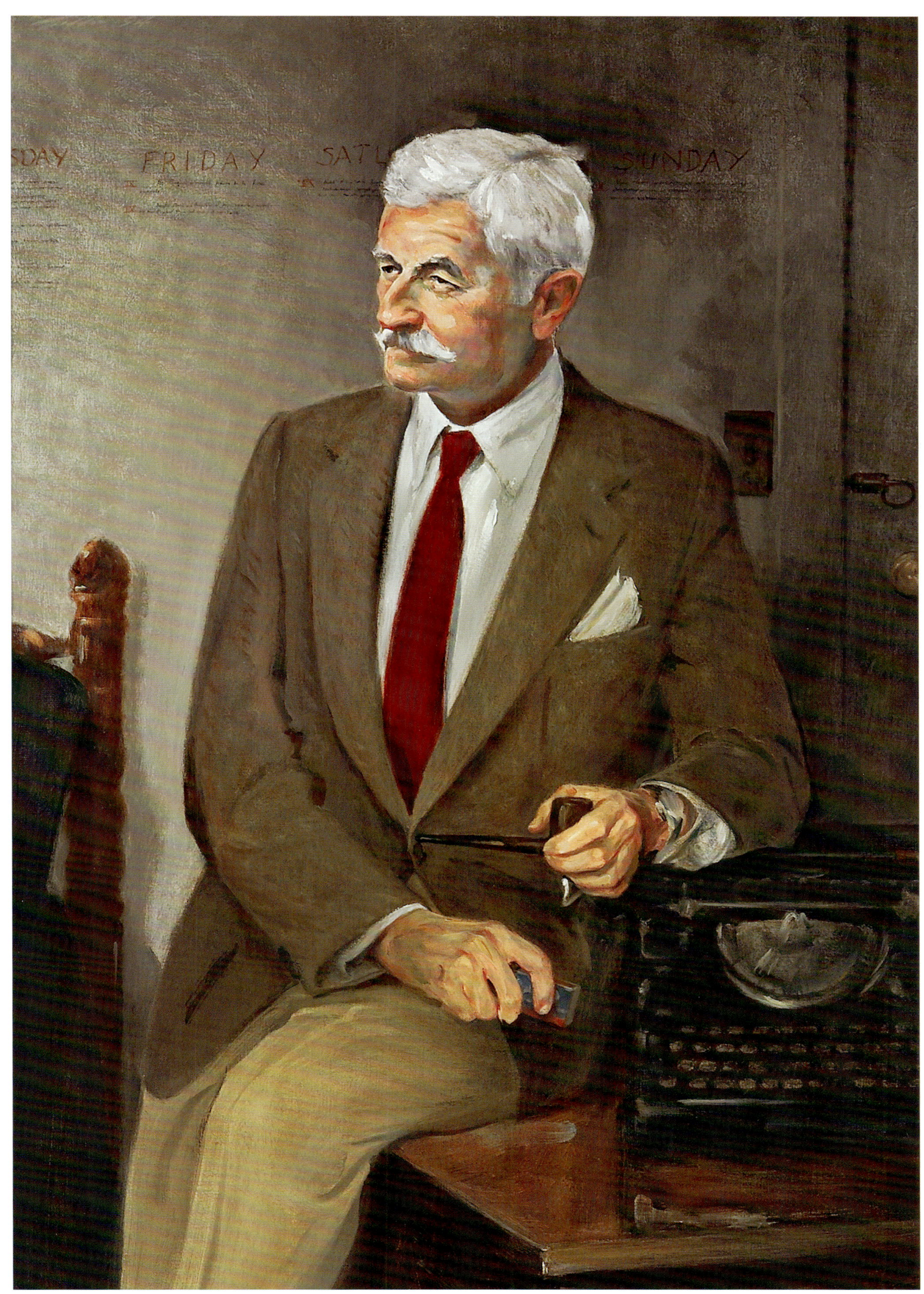

William Faulkner, 1994, oil on canvas, 41 x 28. *Collection of the Museum of Mississippi History, Mississippi Department of Archives and History, Jackson.* 1994.7.1.

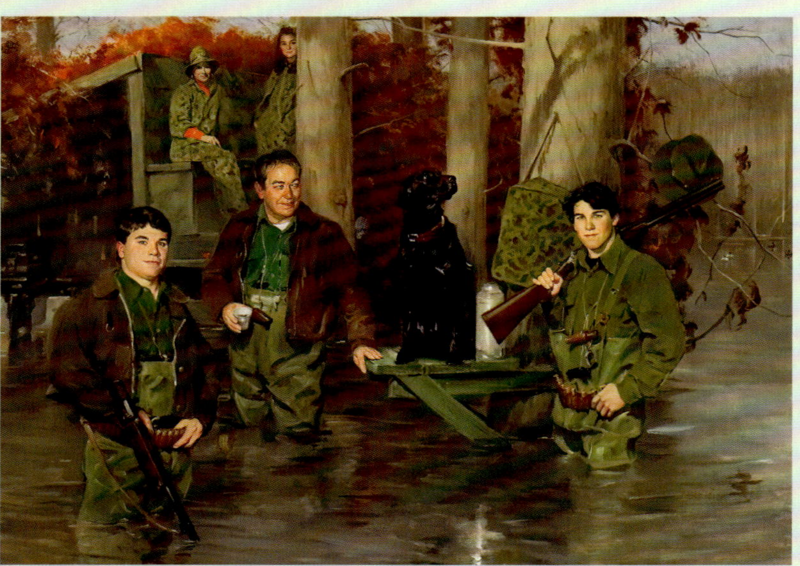

The North Hole, 1991. oil on canvas. 53 x 74½. *Collection of Mr. and Mrs. John Cooper, Jr., Bella Vista, Arkansas.*

In simple terms, traditional portraits like Bouldin's are convincing likenesses that preserve personal identity and show the subject's status or position. A portraitist's unique vision invariably emerges in his art, revealed by his distinctive process, abilities, and aesthetic sense. Commission portraiture is a collaborative arrangement, in which the painter fashions an image that not only satisfies his client, but also his own creative goals. Before beginning a portrait, Bouldin engages the sitter in casual conversation, listening for clues about his or her work and interests, and looking for revealing gestures, idiosyncrasies, or attributes that he may weave into the painting. Following in the footsteps of perceptive portraitists such as Velasquez or Sir Henry Raeburn (1756–1823), Bouldin reaches beyond appearance to find, distill, and reveal the essence of each individual.

Bouldin's purposeful compositions are the structures upon which his portraits are built. His nuanced, dramatic waist-length portrait of *Maestro Simon Kooyman*, circa 1966–1968, is a marvel of simplification. The conductor, standing before his sheet music with arms upraised and baton in hand, looks commandingly over his unseen musicians. The dark, spare background pulsates with broad, painterly strokes that suggest the conductor's vigorous leading gestures and the symphonic strains of the orchestra.

The North Hole, 1991, one of Bouldin's most ambitious and complex works, is also a narrative about an American family. In this atmospheric, bayou *mise-en-scene*, three men dressed for the hunt stand near each other in the foreground, as two women peer from the duck blind beyond. The figures strike casual postures, but the dog's intent, upward gaze portends the ensuing activity. Composed of a lively network of horizontal, vertical, and diagonal rhythms, and rendered with vigorous brushwork, Bouldin's intriguing painting exudes an air of expectancy.[3]

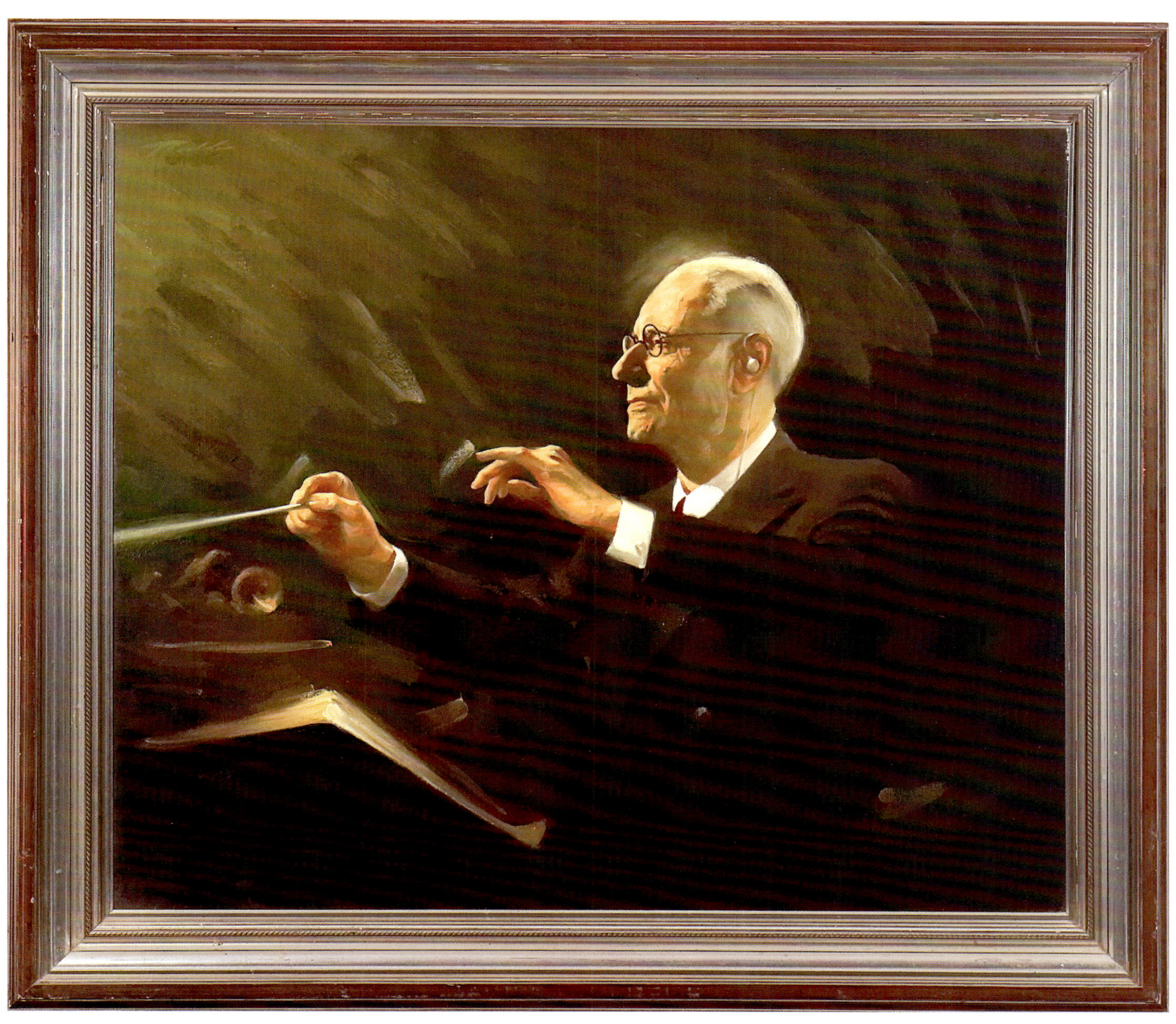

Maestro Simon Kooyman, circa 1966-1968. oil on canvas. 41 x 48.

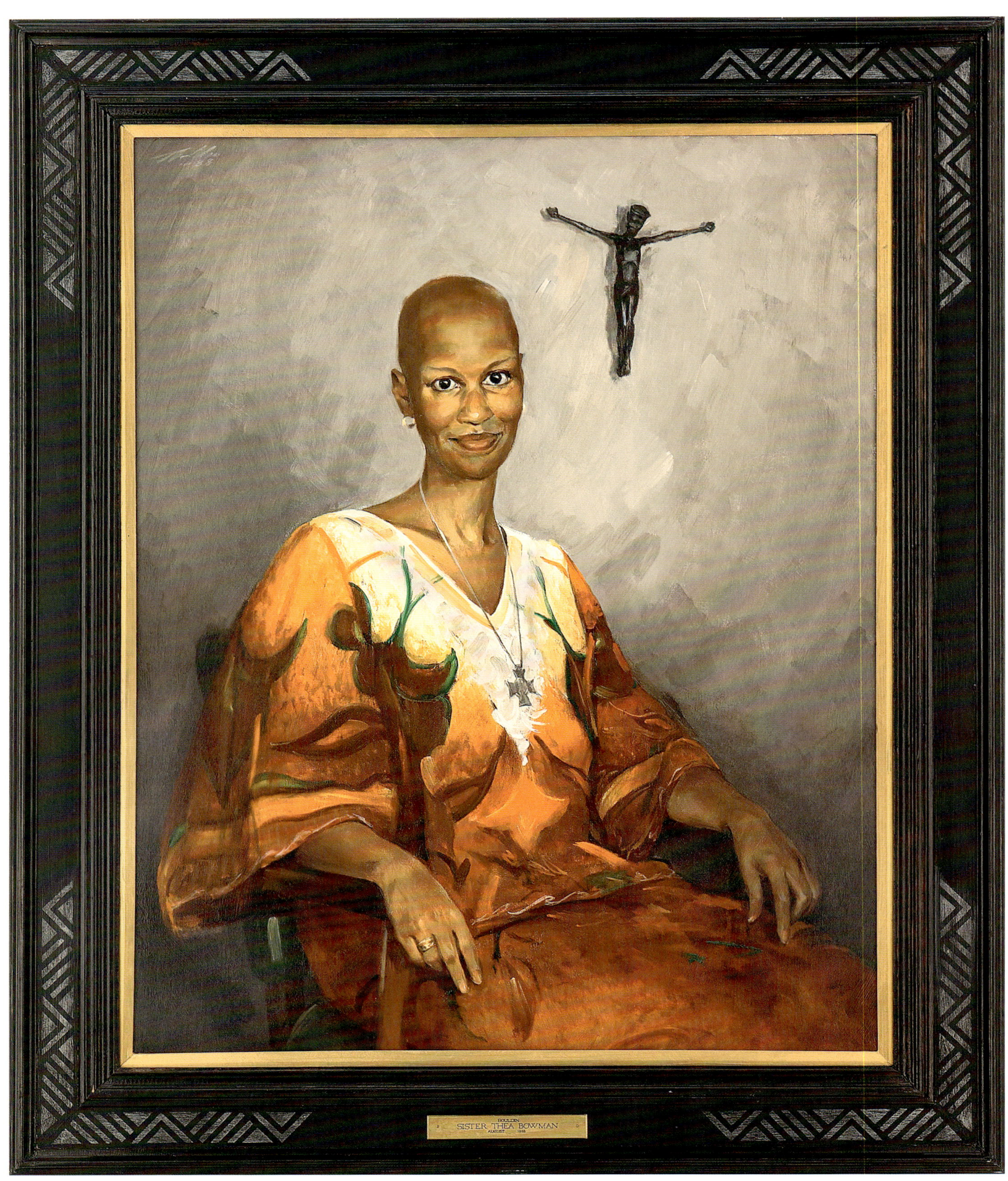

Sister Thea Bowman, 1988. oil on canvas. 43 x 34. *Collection of Roman Catholic Diocese of Jackson, Mississippi.*

Thea Bowman, a sister of the Roman Catholic Diocese of Jackson, proved to be one of Bouldin's most unforgettable subjects. Knowing that she was dying, the painter assumed that he would encounter a fragile, elderly, white-haired nun. Instead, he found a vibrant, engaging woman who was "full of energy," much younger than he expected and, due to the effects of chemotherapy, bald. She surprised and delighted Bouldin by singing selections from opera during the portrait sessions. In his portrait of *Sister Thea Bowman*, 1988, the artist shows the nun seated in a three-quarter pose close to the picture plane, dressed in a flowing, colorful dashiki, and beaming at the viewer with sparkling eyes and broad smile. The cross she wears around her neck and the black crucifix that hangs on the wall nearby are emblematic of her sustaining faith. Rather than a portrait of a dying woman, this painting is a powerful affirmation of her life.

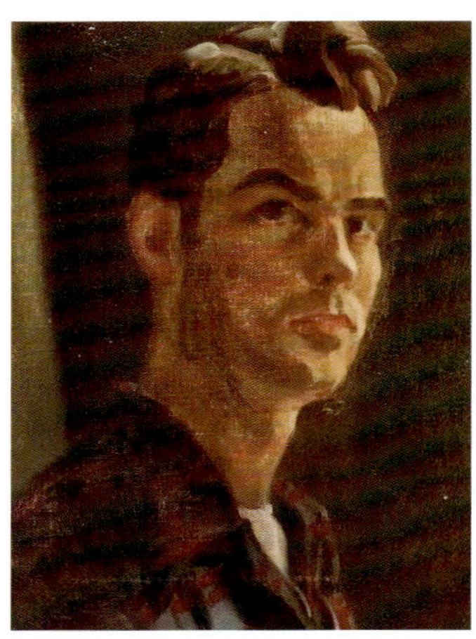

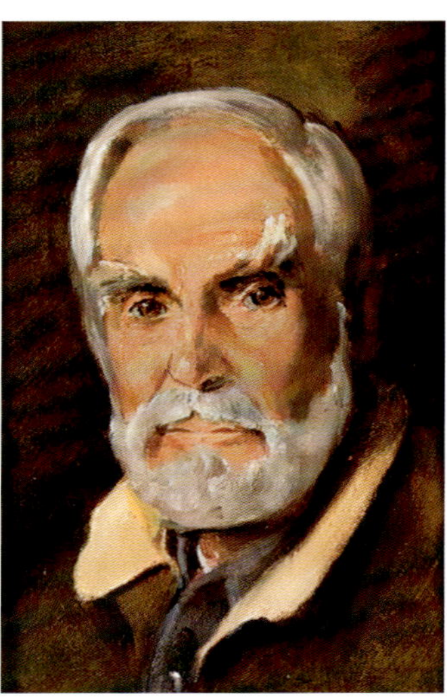

Self-Portrait, 1949. oil on canvas. 17 x 13.

Self-Portrait, 2006. oil on canvas. 9 x 6. *Collection of Mr. and Mrs. Freeman Randolph and Helen Bouldin Jones, Charlotte, North Carolina.*

The Man in the Mirror

A less recognized but significant aspect of Bouldin's art is self-portraiture, a practice that he has continued for more than half a century. While the portrait work mirrors the painter's ability to reveal the essence of his sitters, the self-portraits reflect his candid inquisitiveness about himself. Usually painted in just a few hours, these small canvases reflect his evolution as an artist and his changing countenance, and provide glimpses into their creator's mind.

Bouldin's intense, piercing gaze is the central focus of his earliest self-portrait, completed in 1949, shortly before his return to Mississippi from Connecticut. The painting's pensive tone is underscored by the somber, claustrophobic background and the moody interplay of light and shadow across his features. This introspective work would seem to reflect Bouldin's growing discontentment with illustration at the time, and the heavily scraped surface evokes his struggle to finish the work.

The colorful *Self-Portrait in the Manner of Van Gogh*, 1952, in contrast, sounds an upbeat note. In this series work, Bouldin depicts himself as a handsome young man, with generous strokes of paint delineating his features. Though his head is turned slightly away from the picture plane, his eyes are fixed on the viewer. Casually dressed in shirt and jacket, with hat set atop his dark hair at a jaunty angle, the artist brims with vitality. The luminous yellow background that surrounds the figure suggests a sun-drenched, *plein-air* environment, and renewed optimism.

Successive images from later decades document inevitable physical changes in Bouldin's visage, as well his growing mastery of the painter's craft, but none is more eloquent than a recent, quietly dramatic self-portrait from 2006. The viewer not only sees the venerable artist's physical appearance but also comes to understand his outlook at this stage of his life. The decades are visible in his receding hairline, snowy beard and bushy eyebrows, and in the creases across his brow. But more importantly, the liquid eyes that firmly engage ours evince the confidence, wisdom, and the satisfaction of a man who has found, and lived, his life's calling.

---

1 *Paul Valéry, "On Portraits,"* Faces of Impressionism: Portraits from American Collections (*The Baltimore Museum of Art, in association with Rizzoli International Publications, 1999*), *37*.

2 *Bouldin's wife was enrolled in medical school at the time, and had been supplied with a set of human bones for study purposes. The artist exhaustively studied the bones to learn how they fit together and supported the range of human movement. From this work, he created an extensive set of isometric drawings for his anatomy book.*

3 *Because of the logistical difficulties posed by the outdoor setting, Bouldin worked from his own photographic sources. In a telephone conversation May 27, 2008, he recalled arranging and photographing the subjects on site, while standing in a boat steadied by his son, Jason. Because the family's daughter was absent from the sitting, the mother assumed separate poses for the two female figures. Later, using a photographic image supplied by the family, the artist added the daughter's head to the second figure.*

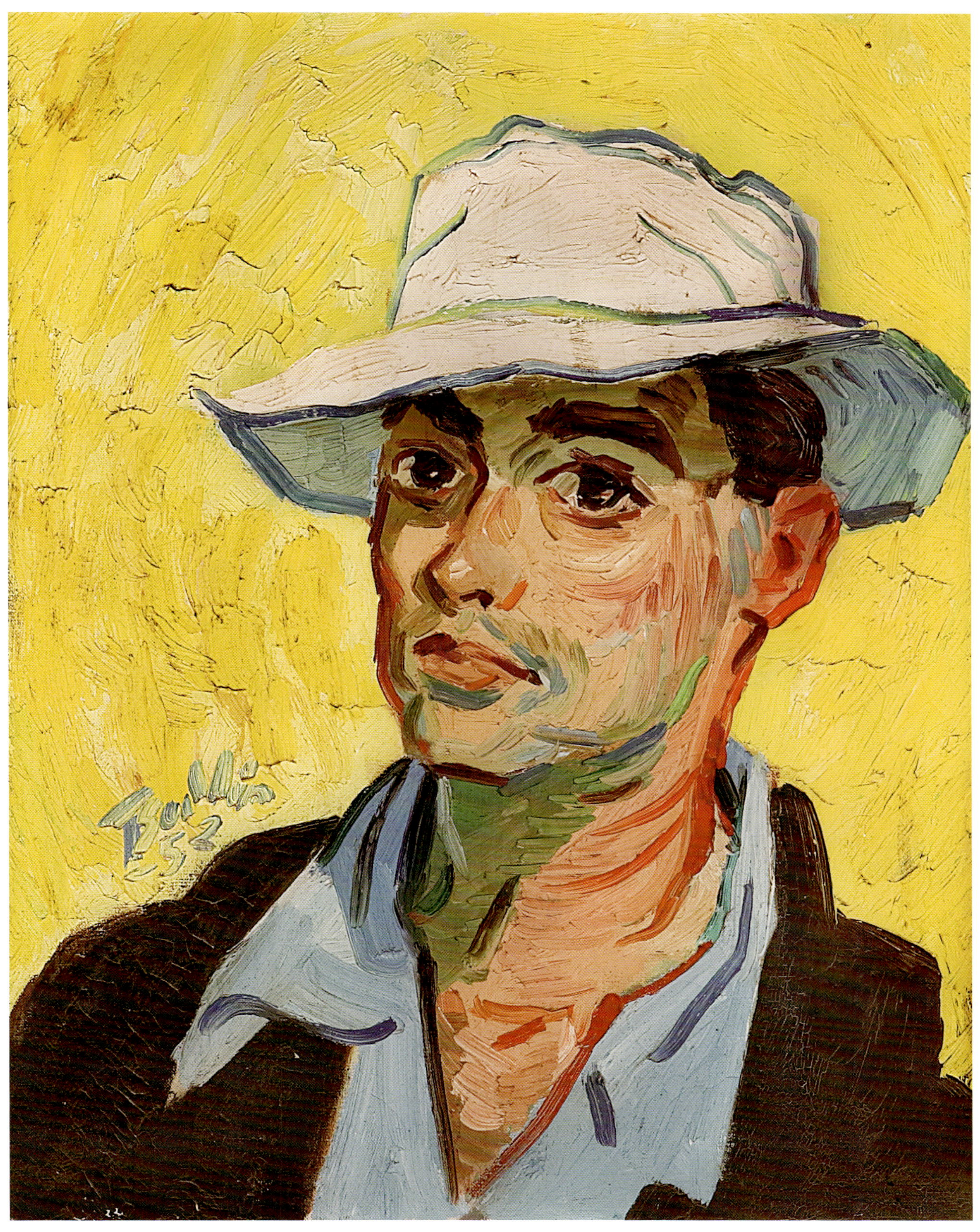

Self-Portrait in the Manner of Van Gogh, 1952. oil on canvas. 22 x 18.

Marshall Bouldin: In His Own Words

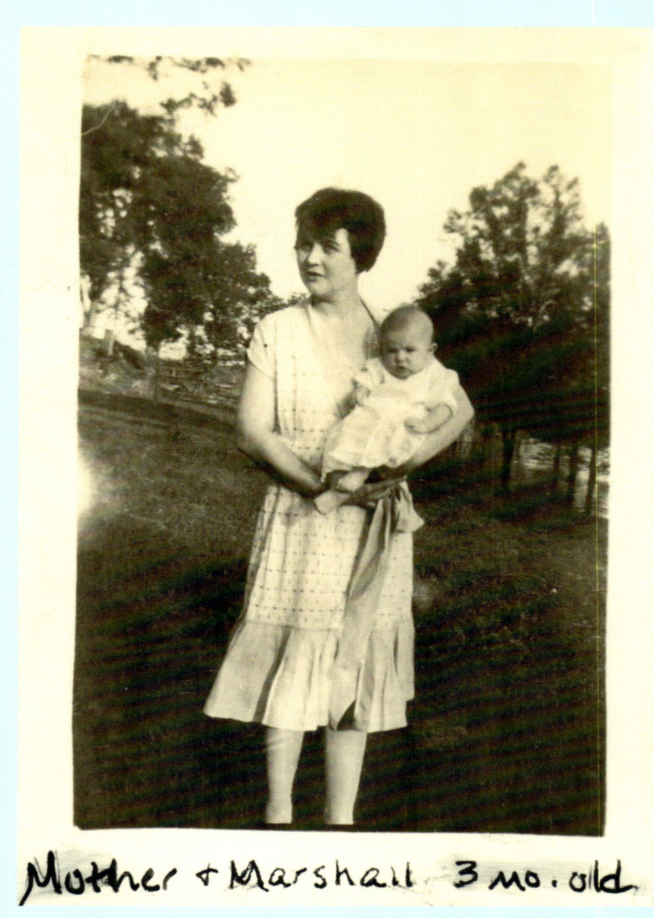

Laurenze Cooper Bouldin with her son, Marshall Bouldin III.

"I look back and I see things how they happened, when they happened, and why they all happened, and all that points to making me into an artist."

From Dundee to Chicago Well, first I was born.... When I started out with my peers, children same age as I was, I didn't get along with them very well. I couldn't keep up with them so I was sort of left out with things, and that sort of made me feel low. I had to learn how to take in a lot of my own emotions at an early age. I found out that I liked to draw. About the only attention I got from someone—everybody likes to be patted on the back—an old person would come along and would pat me on the head and say, "Oh look at the little boy, he draws." That gave me the greatest thrill in the world. Well, then I started learning when I was drawing, when I started school, I was excited to take some of my drawings to school. The students I was with were only in the second grade or something, and of course all I got from the students was, "Oh, my brother can draw better than you." And that hurt, it hurt me a lot, you know? So I said to myself that I still wanted to be an artist. There was art instruction, but when I think on it there was no instruction. I took art class, and when I sat in class they would give me a picture and say, "Copy this." They would tell me where I had gone wrong a little but not much; they didn't know a lot about artists.

That's when I decided that I wanted to grow up to be an illustrator like Norman Rockwell. That was my goal. When I got up into high school, it was 1939, and there was really no art in the South. There was a museum in Memphis with a few pictures in it. My mother knew I was interested in art so she took me up there. That really turned me on, the few oil paintings that I had seen till I got out of high school. In high school there was a magazine that listed scholarships to all the different schools, and I decided I was going to get myself a scholarship. So, I prepared some drawings and sent them in. Lo and behold, I got a scholarship.

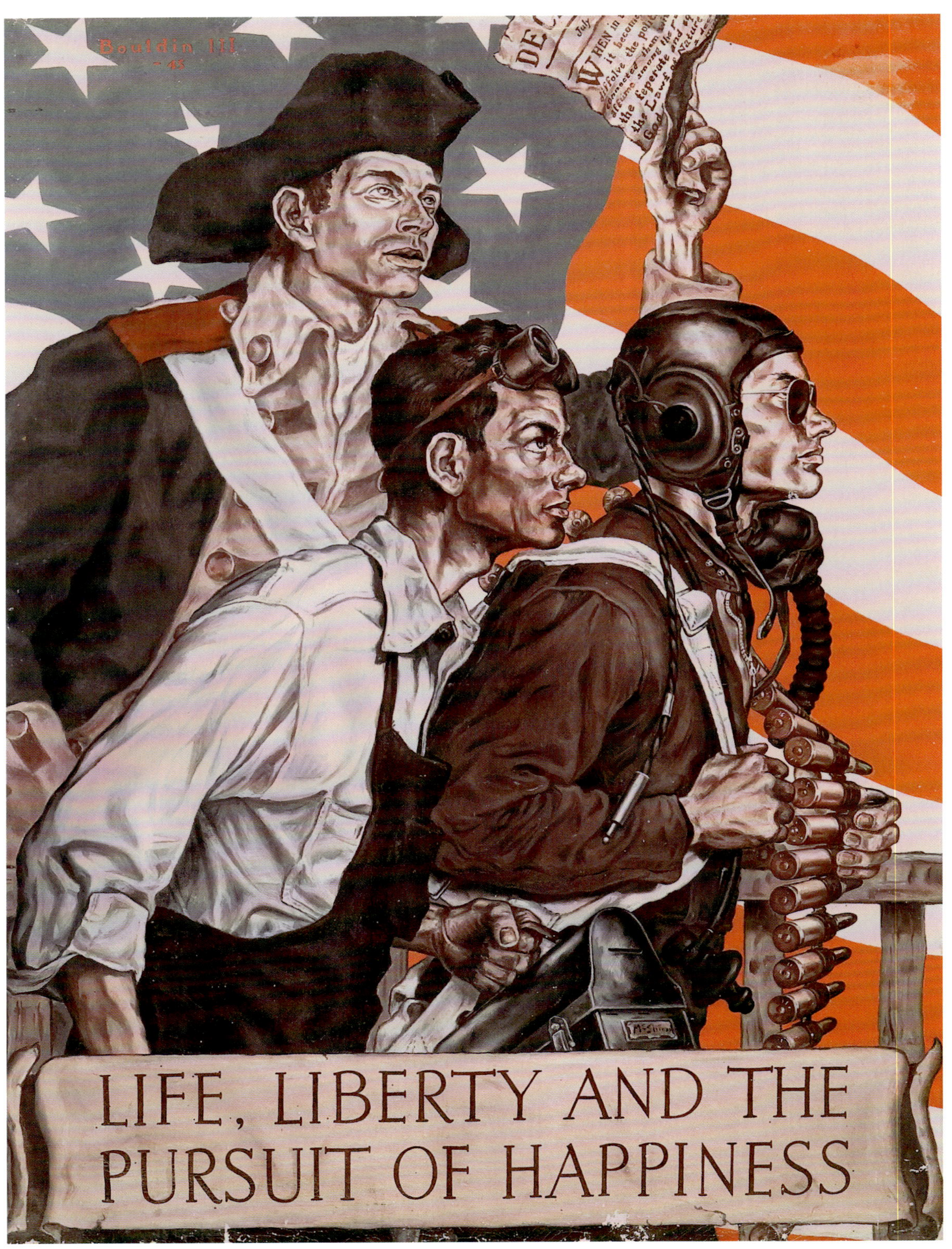

Life, Liberty and the Pursuit of Happiness, 1945. oil on canvas. 37 x 28.

In Chicago

When I got to the Art Institute in Chicago, I said, "Oh, boy I'm gon' learn about art, how to really draw, really paint." Well, I got into that and I found out that they didn't really teach you anything about drawing, they sort of let you draw, but then they didn't give you much instruction. For me, they should have taught me anatomy, how to draw a person, or how to mix colors. I didn't know what a color wheel was. This is a standard thing, and I didn't know what a color wheel was until I quit the Art Institute. My gosh! That's the first thing you want to know about color, how to mix. They kept telling me in the school, "Don't do any of that. That's going by the rules. What you've got to do is be free and just loosen up and just do what you want to do." That's what I did for a really long time, and I just got really bored with it. So I decided I wasn't getting where I wanted to go. But the greatest thing I did learn, which is the greatest thing of value to me, and I think it would be of great value to an art student, is every day at noon time we had an hour off for lunch. The school was in the basement of the Art Institute, so all I had to do was run upstairs and I was in the presence of all these masters. When first I got there I looked at the paintings, there were very few paintings that really, really turned me on because most of them were toward the impressionistic side; they weren't Norman Rockwells. The biggest guy that I saw when I first went in there, before I knew anything about anything, was Caravaggio. He painted very realistically, so realistically that when I learned more it turned me off because it's very much like a photograph, almost. When I went in, the first paintings I saw were Van Gogh, Toulouse-Lautrec, and so forth. I said, "How did all this child's play get into the museum? This is a bunch of junk. But there must be something to them." I was pretty dumb, but I was intelligent enough to see that they must have something to them, or they wouldn't be here. I figured I better find out what it is. So I kept on looking at them. I'd go up and spend fifteen minutes eating my lunch fast and spend forty-five minutes looking at these things that I didn't like very much. Then after about a year or two of them teaching me that I was a bad artist, I figured I would quit and go seek the illustrators and they would teach me.

Becoming An Illustrator

One of the greatest illustrators was a man who I didn't particularly admire his work, but he had the reputation. He [Haddon Sundblom] was the man who invented the Coca-Cola Santa Claus. He painted all of them. He was a big shot, a really big shot. Someone knew him who knew me and they gave me a letter of introduction to him for me to take to him. Now it did not have a date on it, so I thought that I wasn't good enough to show him my things. I'm going to get some things together and then I'll show him.

Now I couldn't get into the army because of my feet, so I went to work at the aircraft factory in Nashville and did blueprints in perspective because the workers did not have the education they have now. They could not read a blueprint to make sure it was put together properly. So what you had to do was draw a picture from the blueprint, in three dimensions with all the screws going in the right holes. So I learned perspective, and that was one of the rules that they did not teach me in school up there. Of course, I still wanted to be an illustrator and I kept making these samples. I'd read that Norman Rockwell got a cover on *The Saturday Evening Post* when he was twenty-one years old. That just impressed me because I was twenty at the time. I wanted to get something published by the time I was twenty-one. They had a paper at the factory; I guess it was every week. Just a newspaper for the factory, and it had photographs of everyone. I went to the editor of the paper and I said I want to paint you something that you can put into your paper. It was in January so I suggested doing something for the Fourth of July since it would be coming up. I got to work and painting my Fourth of July painting, à la Normal Rockwell. That was in 1945. They gave me $25 for it, and I was proud. It was good. I put it with my collection of samples that I would show to Mr. Sundblom.

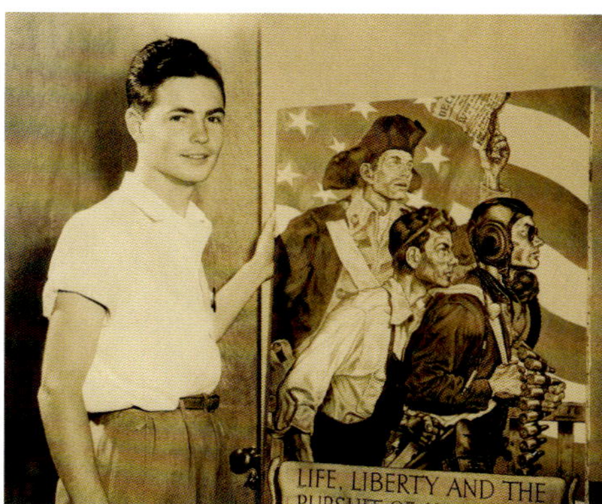

With Life, Liberty and the Pursuit of Happiness, *spring 1945*.

When the war was over and I got out, I went back to Chicago. I made an appointment to see him and talk to him. I walked in, told him my story that I wanted to be an illustrator and there are some things I would like to show you to get your advice. He asked to see them. I brought them out and showed them to him. He looked at them and didn't say a thing; he was quiet. Finally he turned to me and said, "Son, what are you doing now?" I told him I was working at an aircraft factory. He said, "Well I think I would advise you to stay at the aircraft factory," and with that turned and walked away. I tell you what, I went down to the floor. I was crying. I walked out into the streets of Chicago, it was snowing and I was kind of tickled at myself 'cause I was so mad. I shook my fist and said, "I'm gon' show you! I'm gon' show you!"

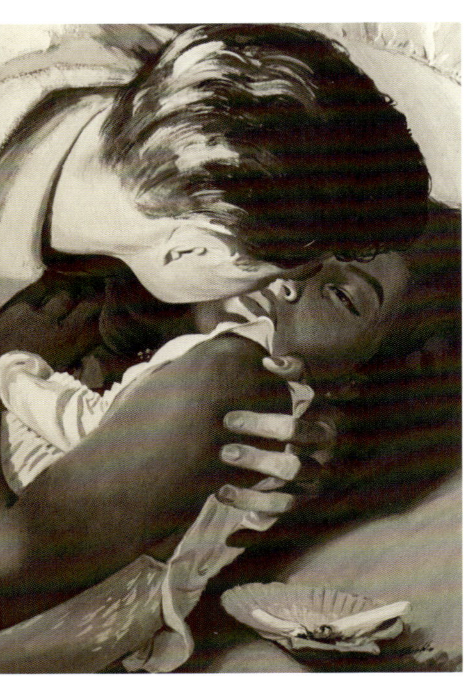

Illustration in which Bouldin used himself and then girlfriend for models, circa 1948–1949.

There was a mecca of illustrators in Connecticut. That's where I was going to go and get a job with one of these illustrators. So I went up there and I did. I got an apprenticeship job, which means I washed brushes, I swept floors, and I ran errands for the artist that I was working for. I sat with his children. But I got exposed to all these illustrators and everything. At that time, well it was really exciting for me to go up there and meet all these people who I had been looking at in these magazines all this time during my high school career, you know, and get to meet them and know them personally. I got to know Harold von Schmidt, who illustrated cowboy stories. It was great to be in his presence and just knowing him there. At that time the television was just coming in, and I could see the illustrators, I witnessed them having a little bit of hard times—magazines were beginning to go out of existence. I did some stories for *Collier's*, I think I did one or two, and for *Outdoor Life*, I did several illustrations for them. I really didn't get the biggest kick out of my illustrations that I thought I would get out of them because they were just stories. But I did make a little bit of a living by doing commercial ads like girls holding up just glasses and smiling. I didn't think that this was really art; it wasn't what I wanted to do. This is not Norman Rockwell. I was unhappy.

Up there I got to know a number of artists who were top notch. [One artist] and I got to be very close friends. One day in talking about this stuff, telling him what I want to do, he put his hand out on one shoulder and said, "Marshall, if you want to get anywhere in this business, you've got to work really hard." That was his way of telling me that I didn't have too much to offer. So I thought about that and figured it was going to be hard for me to make a living at this. About that time I'd been up there about two years. It was then I walked in the Metropolitan Museum—every time I would deliver a painting for these artists to New York I would go to the museum—well, there was a Van Gogh show there. There were about 150 of his works there. It just hit me in the face how great Van Gogh was. It was three years before I thought he was the worst artist in the world. Now, look at all this wonderful color, all these wonderful things. I thought that I could do this and it would be exciting. So much better than pictures of ladies holding glasses up! My father has a farm and said every boy is supposed to grow up and take over the farm. Back in that time you did not have the mechanical farming that you do now you had tenants farming for you, and you had mules. He got up on his horse every morning and rode the whole farm and looked at all the fields, decided what to do with them and then told the tenants what to do and kept them happy. That only took a few hours a day. The rest of the time he spent hunting, fishing, going to the coffee club, and having a good time. I said to myself that I could go back, take over the farm, and I'd have plenty of time to paint. I checked out of there, put all my stuff in my car, and called to say that I was coming home to farm. And they said, "What!?"

"My idea of creativity is when you do something you've never done before, or that you don't know that you can do. We do that all the time. Everybody does it every day."

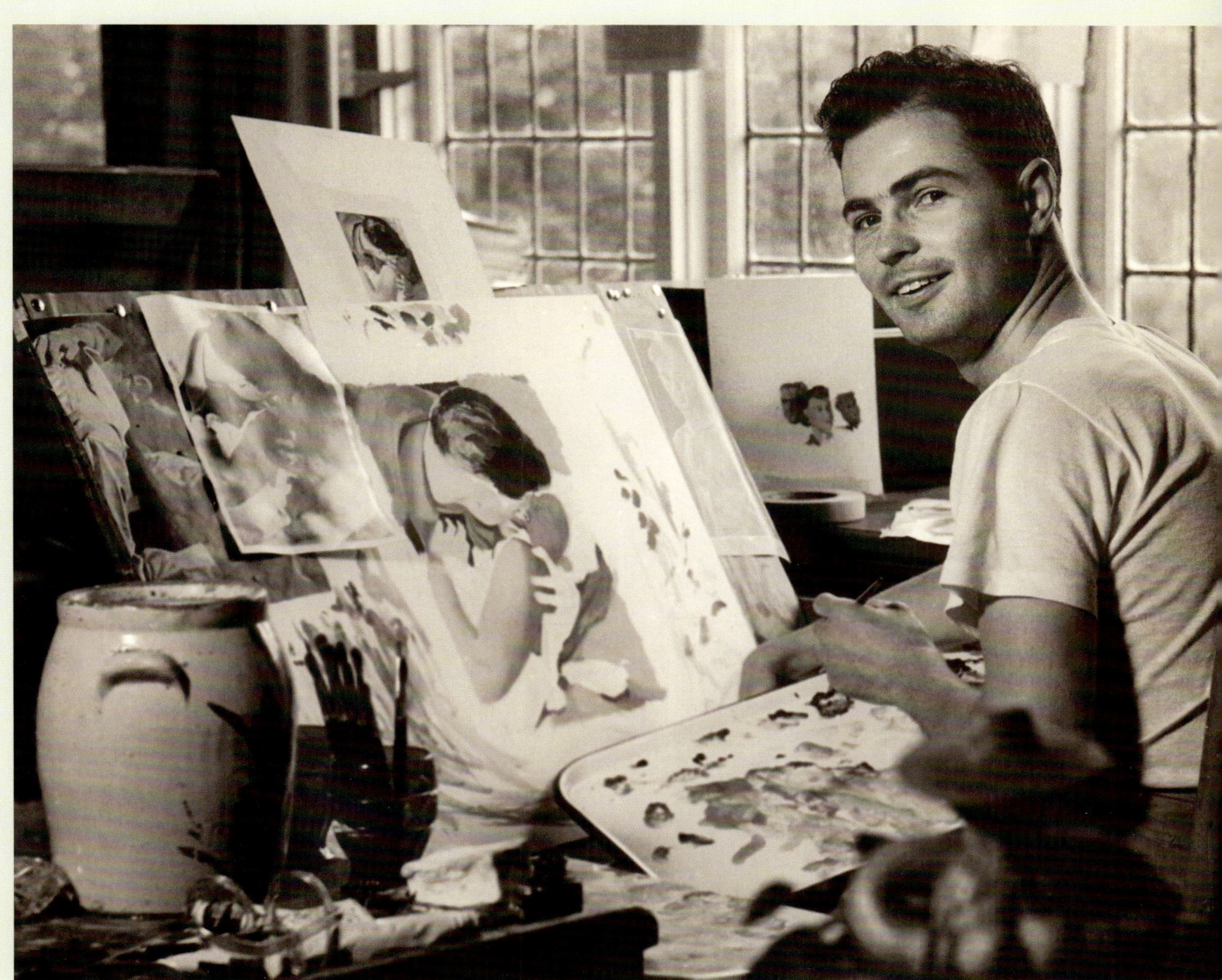

At work on a sample magazine illustration in his Westport, Connecticut, studio, circa 1948–1949.

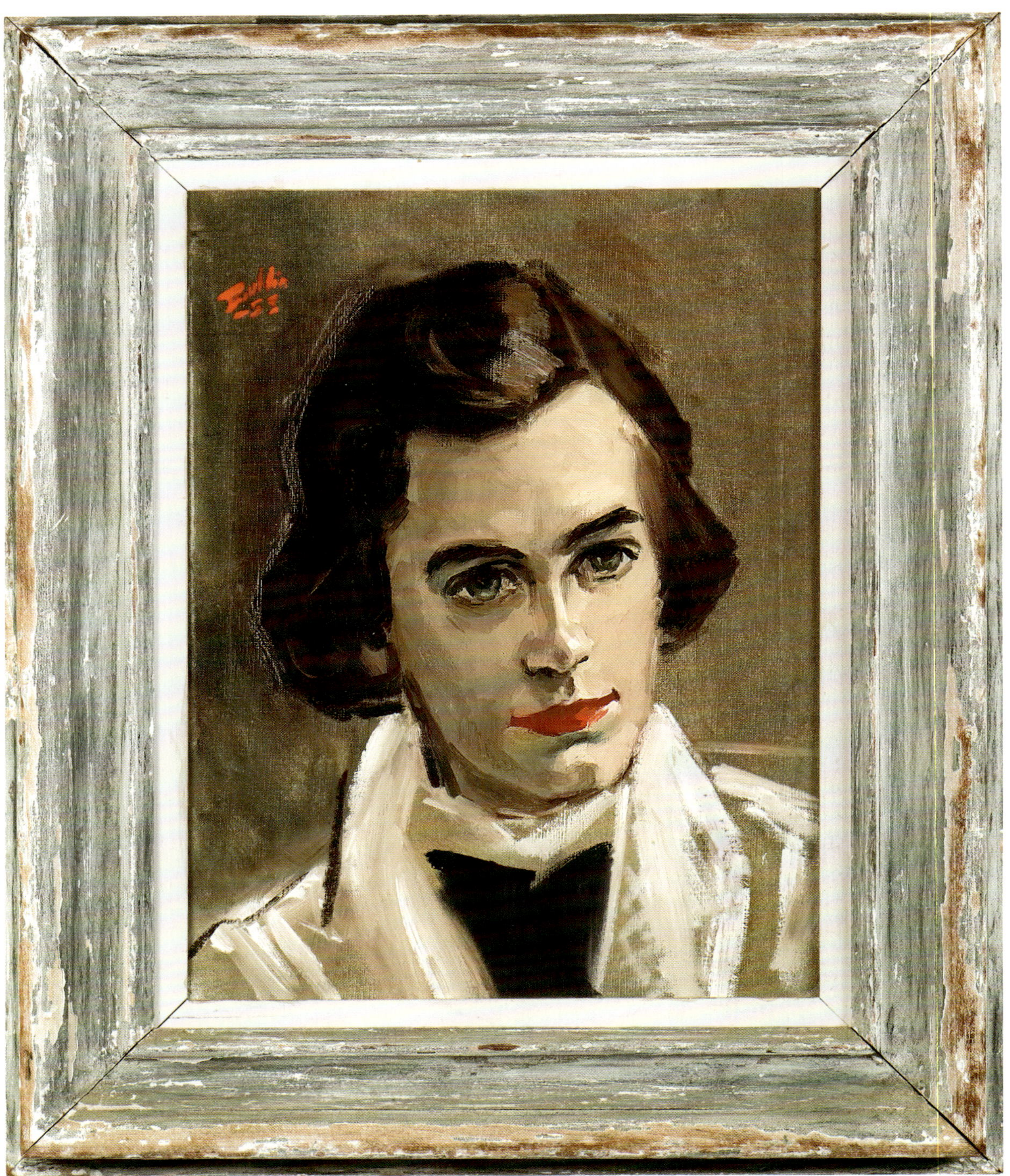

Mel, 1953. oil on canvas. 17 x 13.

Courting Mary Ellen Stribling

The first time I ever saw even a photograph of her was when her father got sick. I went to her house and on the nightstand was her photograph. It was still February at that time and raining. I went with my father over to see her father who was sick in bed. I didn't have anything to say so I was looking around the room, and that's when I first saw her picture over on the dresser. I said to myself, "That looks like a good looking girl to me! I wonder what she's like." I went home and I was sitting down to have supper. My mother had just brought me a beer, and I had just opened it. I asked my mother if they had a daughter, and she said yes, so I asked her to tell me about her. She said that their daughter had been the valedictorian of every class she'd been in, she was a cheerleader, she was a very popular girl, and she was definitely the smartest girl that she had ever met. I took the beer and slapped it down so hard on the table that it foamed out of the top. I said, "Momma, that's the girl I'm gon' marry!" I thought to myself, "I've got to make something out of myself to make her want me." So I thought of the different ways I could date her, and not just have the same old picture show date. Painting a portrait of her from life was one of the things I thought of to do. I started painting her, and I had set up a mirror so she could watch me paint. Well she got to giggling, and I got mad because she wouldn't stay still. Then I tore the mirror down and told her, "Now let's get to work!" I finished the portrait, and we both smiled! That's the only painting I've ever painted of her.

I knew she was who I wanted. She was who I admired. I liked everything about her, and we got along fine. I finally got up enough nerve to ask her to marry me. We were sailing in a sailboat on a moonlit lake on the Fourth of July, skyrockets were going. It was a beautiful thing. And the stars were out, I said, "Well, I'd love to marry you. Can you marry me?" She looked at me and said, "No." I asked her why she couldn't marry me. She said, "Because I want to go to New York and make something out of myself." So that ended that conversation right there. But I still hung in there. It didn't deter me too much. And of course every now and then I kept asking her to marry me.

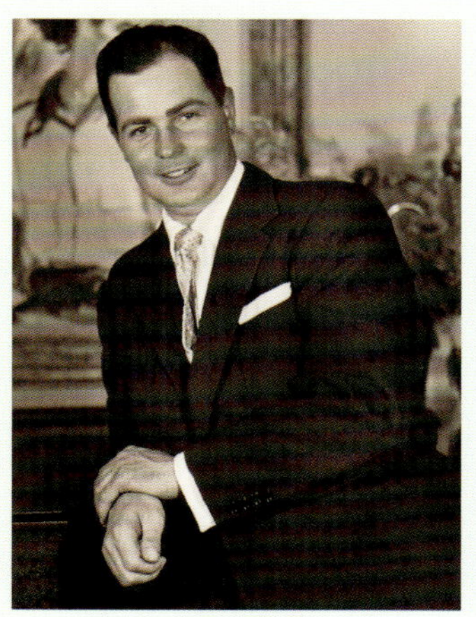

Mary Ellen Stribling's formal portrait of her future husband, Marshall Bouldin III, taken on a date, circa 1953.

One day about three years later, her father got real sick and went to the hospital in Memphis. I would go up every weekend to see her. I wasn't getting anywhere with my marriage proposal, but we really enjoyed each other. Finally I said, "I'm quitting now. I'm ready to go. I've got to ask you this one last time. Marry me, otherwise I'm gone." She said that she'd decided to be a doctor. At that time it was 1953, and there were no women doctors in the South at all, let alone in New York. I thought, "What am I going to do now?" I said, "I'll make a trade with you. If you will marry me and live with me a year, try it out and see how we get along, if you still want to be a doctor, I will do everything in my power to help you be a doctor." She said yes, which made me very happy, and of course I quickly forgot about the doctoring business. We had a first year of marriage that was a little rough because she was going and doing. At that time it was common for women to stay home and do the house work, the washing and the ironing and the cooking. That just wasn't her cup of tea.

The Girl I Married

One night exactly a year later, I was getting ready to go to bed and heard this story on the black and white television about this woman who was a doctor in England. She had quit her doctoring to get married, and her husband had gone to Africa, so she went to Africa. I was in the bathroom and listening, and I thought that didn't sound too good. I came in to go to bed, and she was sitting up along the side of the bed with her arms crossed looking at the television. The program had just gone off, and she was still staring at it. I sneaked into my side of the bed. I glanced over, and she hadn't moved for a half an hour. I guess I had drifted off to sleep. I woke up about two o'clock in the morning, and the television was still on. She was still sitting there. I thought, "What the hell am I going to do now?" I thought about my promise and the doctoring business. I said, "It's time for you to start becoming a doctor." And with that, she came alive. We didn't tell anybody what we were doing, but Monday morning we went to Ole Miss to find out what she had to do to get in, but you see they didn't have a medical school at that time. She needed one more subject; that was chemistry. So I think she went to Itawamba Junior College or something up in northwest Mississippi. We were all excited because we had it all worked out to where she could do it. So at the end of the week, Sunday night, we made dinner and invited the family over, and they knew something was going on. There were candles out on the table and everything. They thought we were going to announce a baby, and when we told them what we were doing, that was really something. My father, who is a really old farmer, just couldn't get in to any of this stuff. He said, "What!? That's the damned-est thing I ever heard in my life." Her mother said it wasn't going to work. I love telling this story. We went to University of Tennessee, where the medical school had just started, and applied there. The first three days we found out that she could get the whole thing in three years. At that time they published class standings in the school newspaper. Well, for the first three months her name was at the list above fifty-seven other men in that class. I got sorta proud of it. So I went to Dad and showed it to him. He looked at the paper and said, "Humph!" and threw the paper down.

Things kept on happening like that for three years. She was top notch in her class. That's when Dad came back to me and actually apologized to me. Then graduation came. My father was not one to sit through graduation talks. He had to get up to go to the bathroom; he was standing there taking a smoke. While he was smoking a man came in, very talkative. He said, "You know my son has been in this class, he's as smart as he can be. I'm so proud of him I don't know what to do. There's only one thing wrong. There's a girl in that class who beat him every time!" And with that, my father took a long drag off his cigarette and flicked it into the wastebasket and said, "That's my daughter," and turned and walked out. What a story. That's the girl I married.

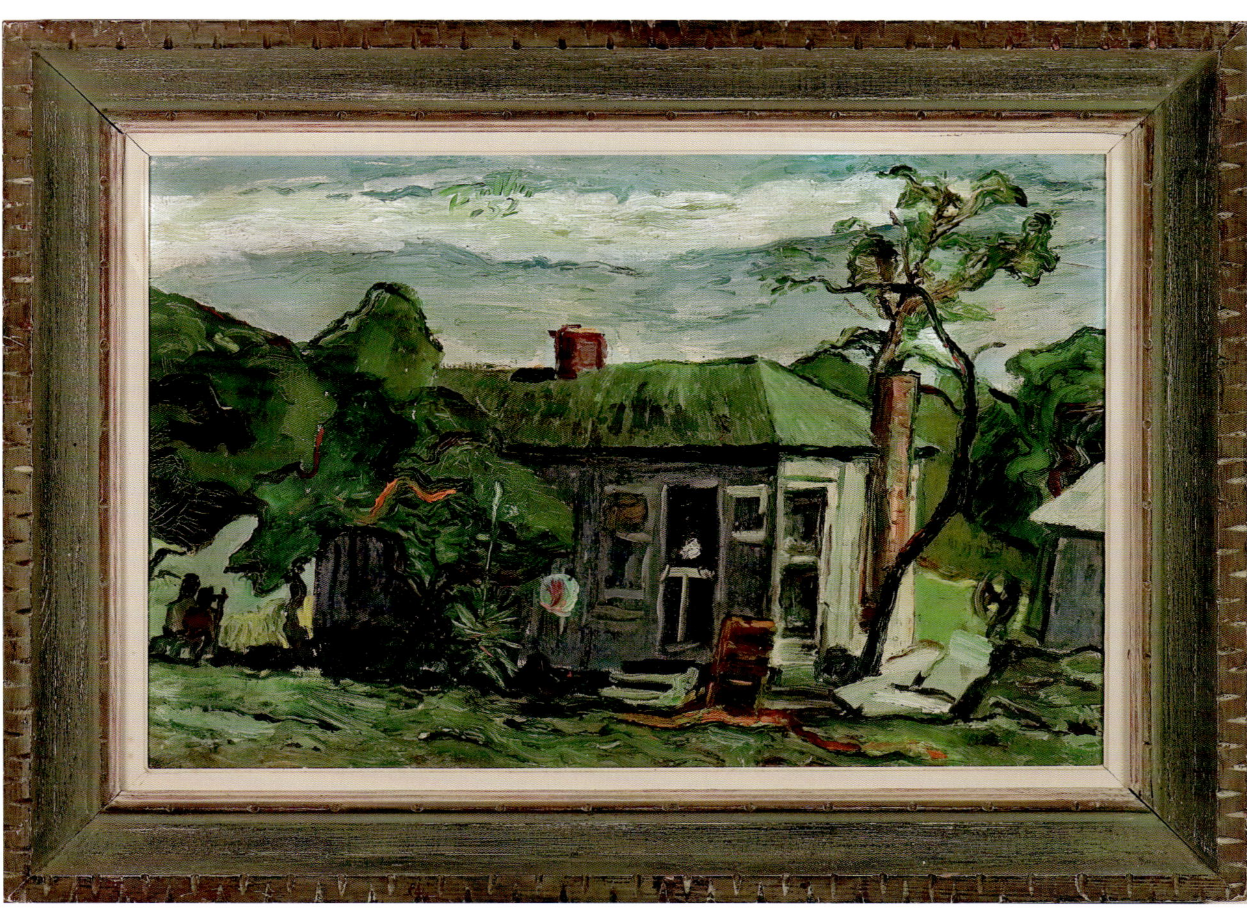

Cabin on Strib's Place, 1952. oil on canvas. 20 x 30.

Developing A Style

So I got here and started painting, à la Van Gogh. I painted like that for two years until I got sick of Van Gogh. But the whole time I was painting I would read a book at night on artists' lives. I got into Toulouse-Lautrec, then Renoir. I painted like them just for fun. I did a little painting of a piano teacher who had one hand paralyzed. I knew her, she had taught my sister music. I got a big kick out of it, but I still didn't think about portrait painting until I read this book on Sargent. By that time I had worked through Renoir and early Picasso. Then I got into my Jackson Pollack period of throwing paint, that was interesting, but I got bored with it pretty fast. I started painting like Franz Kline who was doing black and white abstractions. At that time I was sort of confused, I was bored with art and didn't know what to do. My wife Mel was going to medical school at that time. I saw how happy she was and I was just miserable. I didn't want to paint, I said, "What's the matter with you?" So I figured I would get my paintings out and look at them and maybe that will give me some inspiration. I got these paintings out of the barn, they had dust all over them. I washed them off with a garden hose when all of the sudden I had an epiphany. I started lining them up in order, starting with Van Gogh, going on to Toulouse-Lautrec, to so and so to, then Matisse then Picasso, then Franz Kline and my black and white abstractions there and I said, "Look at that!" I followed the progress of modern art, unconsciously. What is different about these things? It looked like to me that they were leaving out things. As you go, you leave out more and more and more stuff. Until you get down here and what can you do next? While all this is going on in my mind it came out in the newspaper that a painting that had won the biggest show at the Art Institute of Chicago which was

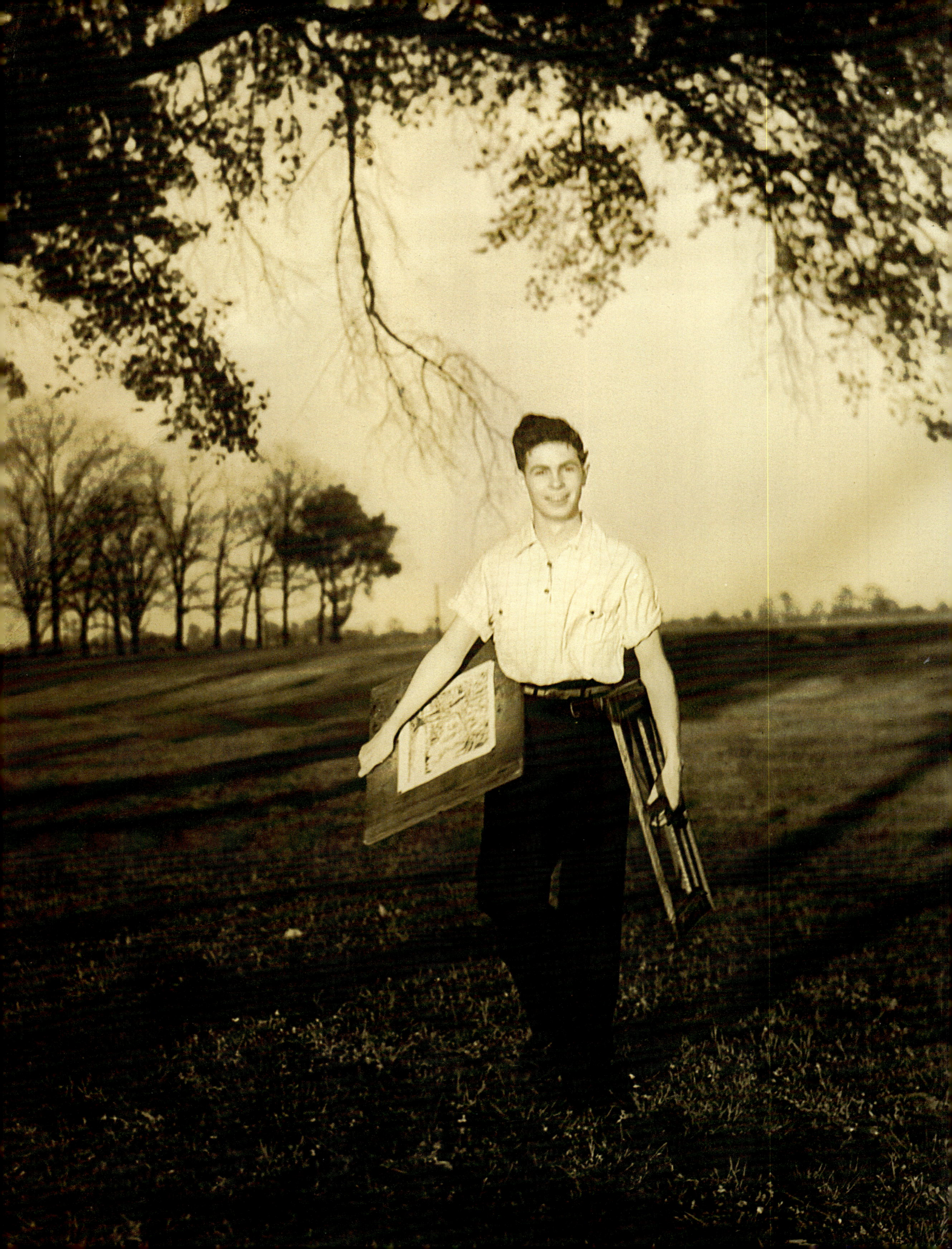

completely black. When I saw that I thought well all you can leave out is the canvas now. This thing has got to turn around, and I don't know what's going to happen next. Incidentally, I have seen that black painting; it's still hanging in the Art Institute and it's a wonderful painting because of the texture in it that didn't show up in the photo. It's still a great painting, but I didn't have enough nerve to do this painting that was completely black. Well anyway, that's about the time I read a book on John Singer Sargent. I read it and I said, "Hey this looks like a pretty good life to me." I could see all the illustrators I had admired going out of business because magazines were drying up and I said, "Well I'm in the wrong profession," but hey, everyone wants to see themselves and everybody wants to see realism, and at that time I wanted to see it. I was in Memphis and I saw this Henry Raeburn portrait and I said, "That's a portrait, and it's like Norman Rockwell, but it's better because it has some quality in it." I got excited when I looked at it even though I didn't know at that time why I was getting excited over it. So something had to turn around. I started painting again, getting some of the work in doing portraits of people, asking them to sit for me. We'd spend about an hour and a half time in the morning when we weren't doing much farming. I had a good time doing it, and then I thought, "Wow, maybe I could do portrait painting." That's when my father said that if I could paint a white person then I could make some money at this. Right at that time, after my father said that, this man in town asked me if I could paint his portrait. I said no I can't I've never painted a real portrait. He said he'd give me a hundred dollars and I said, "What? I can't paint! Let me go home and practice." Now, I want that hundred dollars, so I went home and tried to paint a realistic head of a little white person, my

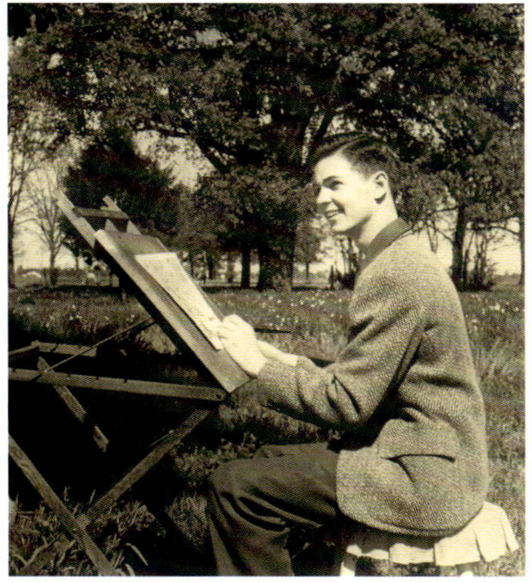

(left and right)
Publicity photographs, circa 1940, that announced Bouldin's scholarship to attend the Art Institute of Chicago.

sister. And I fell flat on my face. I kept thinking of these wonderful Van Goghs and the other things, but I couldn't paint what I wanted to paint, and that really upset me. When I thought about it, I thought about Mel and all we were learning, I thought about the aircraft factory and the perspective drawings, and I went to the library to get some books on art. I found a book that had been published in 1895. In that book I found a color wheel—it was the first time I had ever seen one. Gosh, this makes a lot of sense. Then the book showed anatomy. I said, "If I knew what a bone looked like I could do it." And that's what got me all excited and when I said that I was going to teach myself about this whole thing. I started studying anatomy.

Self-Taught Portraitist

I came in from farming one afternoon about one o'clock, and I was hot, sweaty, and tired. You know, Mel was going to medical school, and when you go to medical school they give you a box of bones to bring home. Lo and behold, I didn't know anything about that! I walked in from farming there into the bedroom, and there was this skeleton laid out on the bed, and I said, "What!?"

And she told me about the box of bones. I looked at that box and said, "Well why did you take it out on my side of the bed?" which she kind of got a big laugh out of. But I can remember very well, there was all this information out. I picked up the skull, and the skull and jawbone weren't attached. And so I remember working the skull and jawbone in my hand and turning it and looking at it. I said, "Now look, I can turn and draw a brickbat, because I had been doing perspective from blueprints, why can't I draw this if I knew what it was like, so I've got to study anatomy." So with that I went and got me some anatomy books, and I was disappointed because they all just showed blueprints of the skeleton, like the blueprints in the aircraft factory. There were no drawings like those that I'd been making for the aircraft factory from the blueprints, perspective drawings so you could really see what something

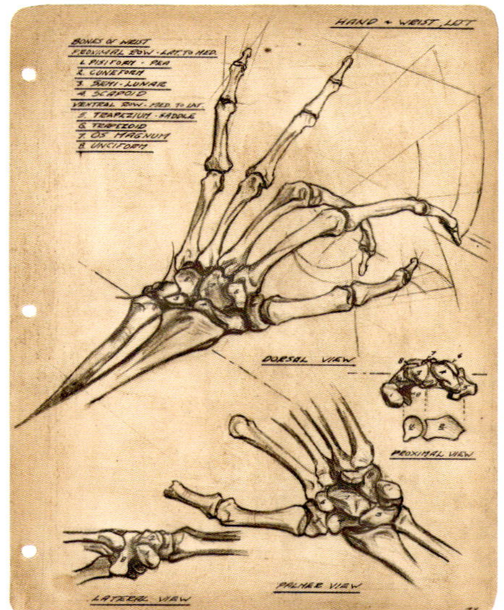

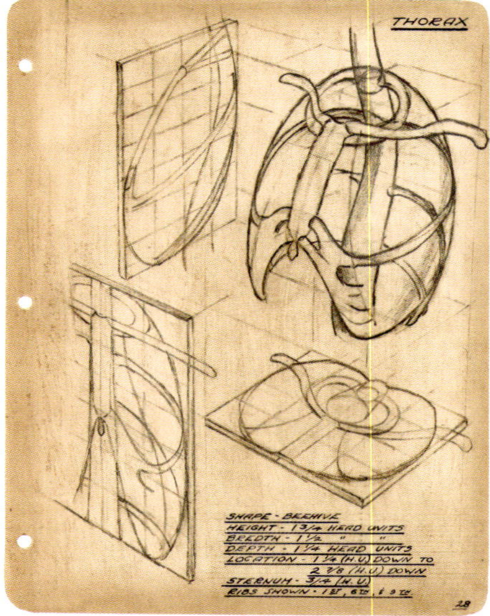

Hand & Wrist, Left, page 73; **Thorax**, page 28; **Skull – Mandible Articulations**, page 4; from anatomy book, circa 1956-1958. graphite and ink on paper. 11 x 8½, each.

SKULL - MANDIBLE ARTICULATIONS

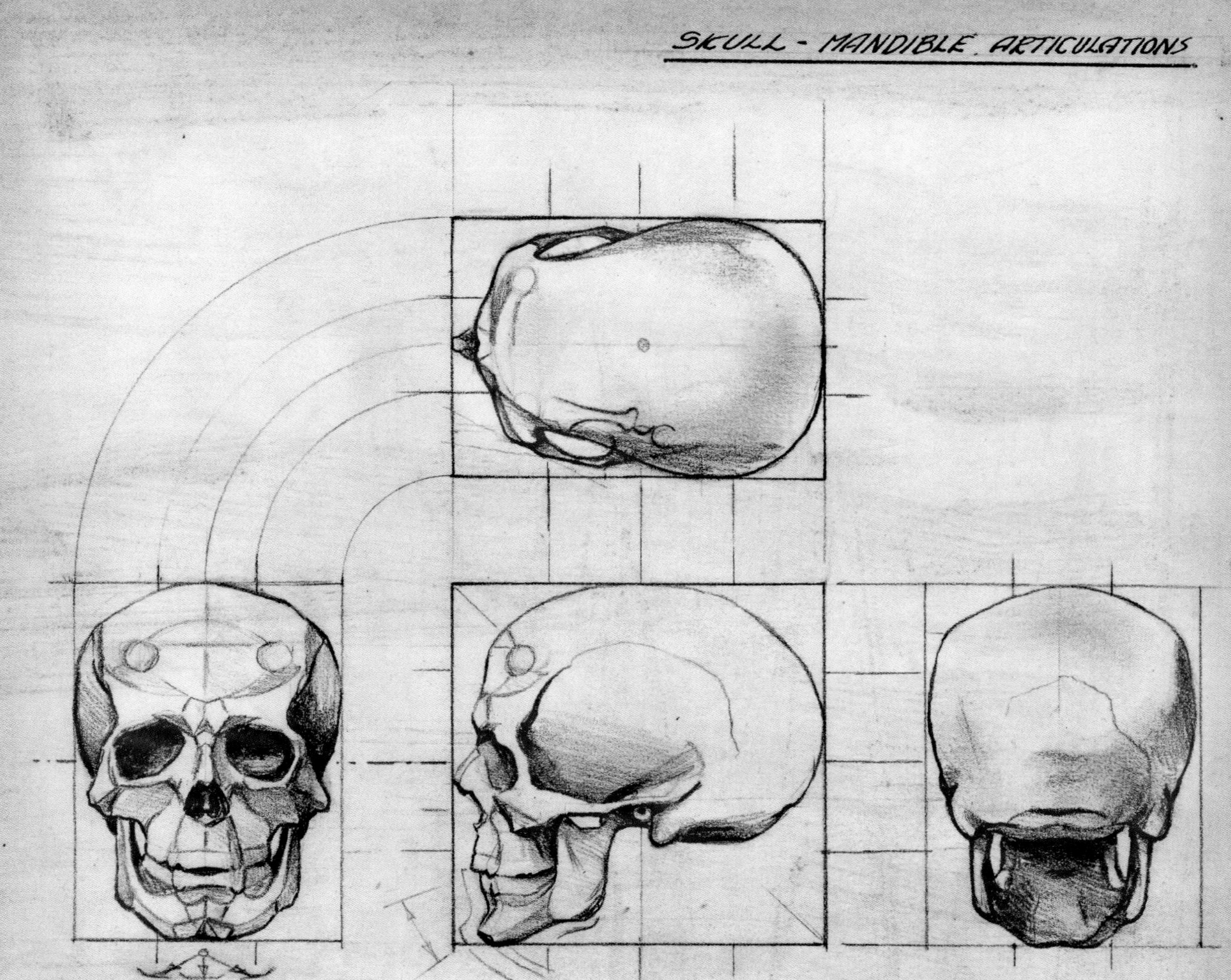

HEIGTH - 1 HEAD UNIT
WIDTH - 3/4 HEAD UNITS
LENGTH - 1 HEAD UNIT
LENGTH OF CRANIUM - 7/8 HEAD UNITS
PIVOT POINT - 1/2 BACK
5/8 DOWN
EAR OPENING - SAME AS PIVOT POINT
EYE LOCATION - 1/2 DOWN
1/3 WIDTH OF HEAD APART (1/4 H.U.)

MANDIBLE ARTICULATIONS -

- MAY BE DROPPED SLIGHTLY
- MAY BE THRUST FORWARD OR RECEEDED
- MAY BE TWISTED HOROZONALLY ABOUT 10° EACH DIRECTION
- MAY BE OPENED ON FLOATING PIVIT ABOUT 25°

4

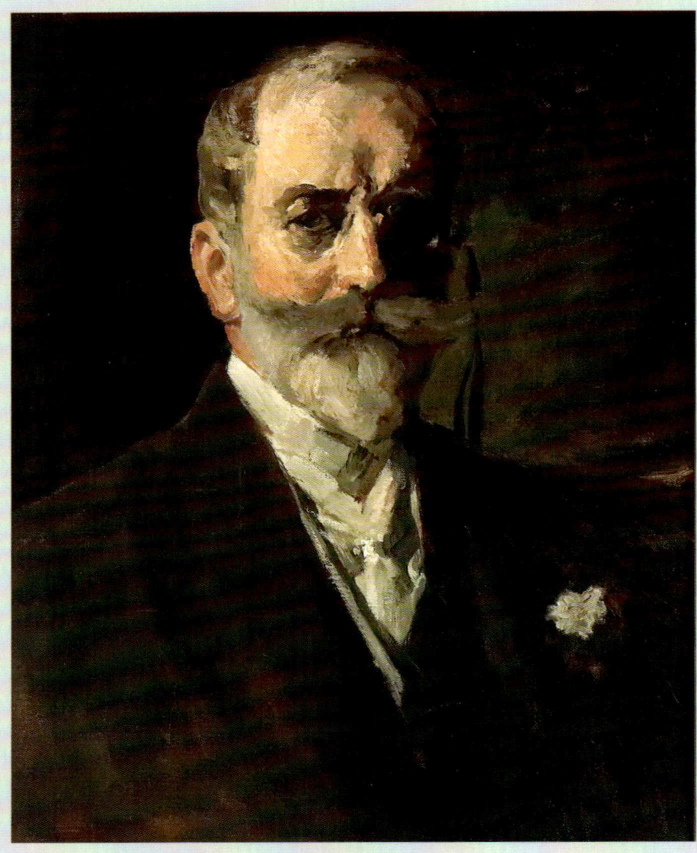

Copy of Self-Portrait by William Merritt Chase, 1960. oil on canvas. 20 x 16.

looked like, so the workers could understand what they were making. There were just no perspective drawings of the skeleton in those books. So I said, "Ah-ha that's what I'm going to do." I got this book that I had been interested in, and I couldn't wait to sneak off from farming to get into this thing, I got this thing together, went through the whole thing from top to bottom, then I got into the mechanics of folds. Made drawings of them, why this works like this on this thing, and so forth. My wife said, "You have turned into a student. There are some people that like to study. You're just going to study and study and never gonna paint again." I said, "No, I know exactly what I'm doing. I'm getting there, and you just hang on." She laughed at me.

Anyway, when I finished all this stuff with the anatomy, I had seen that color wheel and I said, "Now I need to study that color wheel." So I studied the color wheel and I found out mechanically that you can mix this color with this color and get that color. It never changes. You can put a white with it and get this color, or put a little black with it and get that color. And it never changes. It's just like a multiplication table. So I go to mixing colors and saw how that worked and I got to wondering how do I recognize a color, and how do I put these together. So I started mixing these two colors together, and as I came across from this side to that side I had to think of a six point thing, and well, it's mechanical you see. Anyway I got this thing organized to where I had them in a book, or rather in pages, fifteen by twenty-four. I got all through that, but I never stopped to count the colors. But I stopped, counted and multiplied how many swatches I had on each page, and it came out to be about 4,500 colors that I had enjoyed doing.

Now what I've got to do is get these colors down to where I don't even have to think about making them. They just come to me automatically. Then when I got all this stuff done, about two to two and a half years, then I said that I was going to assign myself a thesis to prove to myself that I had learned this.

So I went to Memphis, and I asked if I could go into the museum and copy. So I went in and copied my painting that had inspired me, that's a Henry Raeburn. So I painted that and I got all excited, and I said, "Look! I did that." But I don't want to be limited to painting a realistic painting. I want to be able to handle my colors in another form. So I picked out another painting they had there that was a self-portrait of William Merritt Chase who had done a very thick painting, no details, but it was a very gorgeous painting. So I copied it, and there it is. So I said, "O.K. Now I'm ready to go."

Encouragement from Mel

[Mel had become] a gynecologist. She loved to work. I was painting at the time and was having a lot of trouble. I had just finished a portrait, and she came in and looked at it and said there was something not right with it. I said, "It's not that bad—maybe I can get away with this." Oh, I shouldn't have said that because she turned right in front of me, took her finger and shook it right at my face, and she said, "See these hands?" holding them right in front of my face, "These hands deliver babies! That's my work. Your work is painting portraits. Sometimes I deliver ten or twelve babies in a night, and these hands get so tired I don't think I can do them anymore, but I can't drop a one of them. And you can't drop a portrait." I can still see her finger shaking. That's the way it was from then on. And she would come in and start critiquing my paintings. She would tell me that there was something wrong, and I wouldn't see it. Invariably I would deliver the painting, and the people would zero in on the point that she had brought up to me. So it finally got to be that the boys were beginning to grow, and the story was, "How does Daddy paint a portrait? He paints it then he runs it by Momma." The reason is, it's mostly left brain. She knows what looks right and what looks wrong. She's right in that department. I tell you what, our marriage has gotten better and better and better.

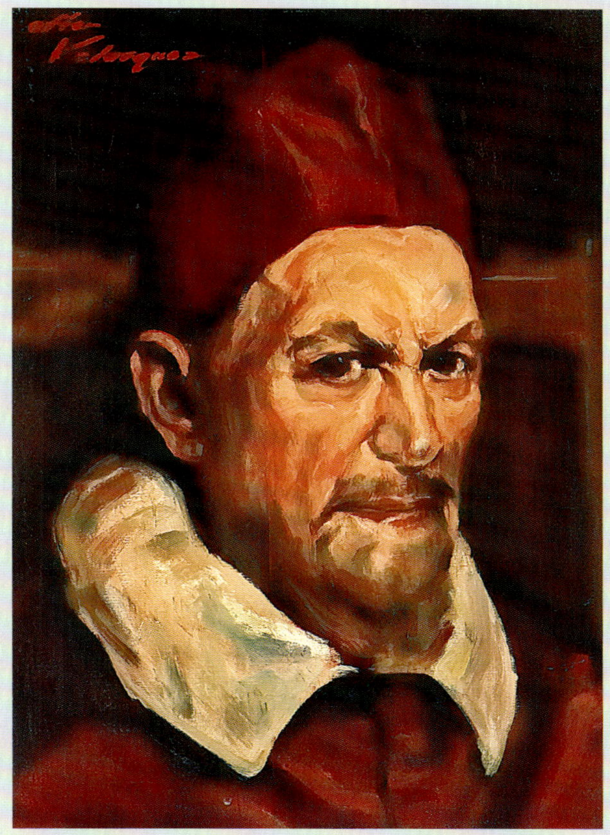

Copy of Pope Innocent X by Diego Velasquez,
circa 1958. oil on canvas. 18 x 13.

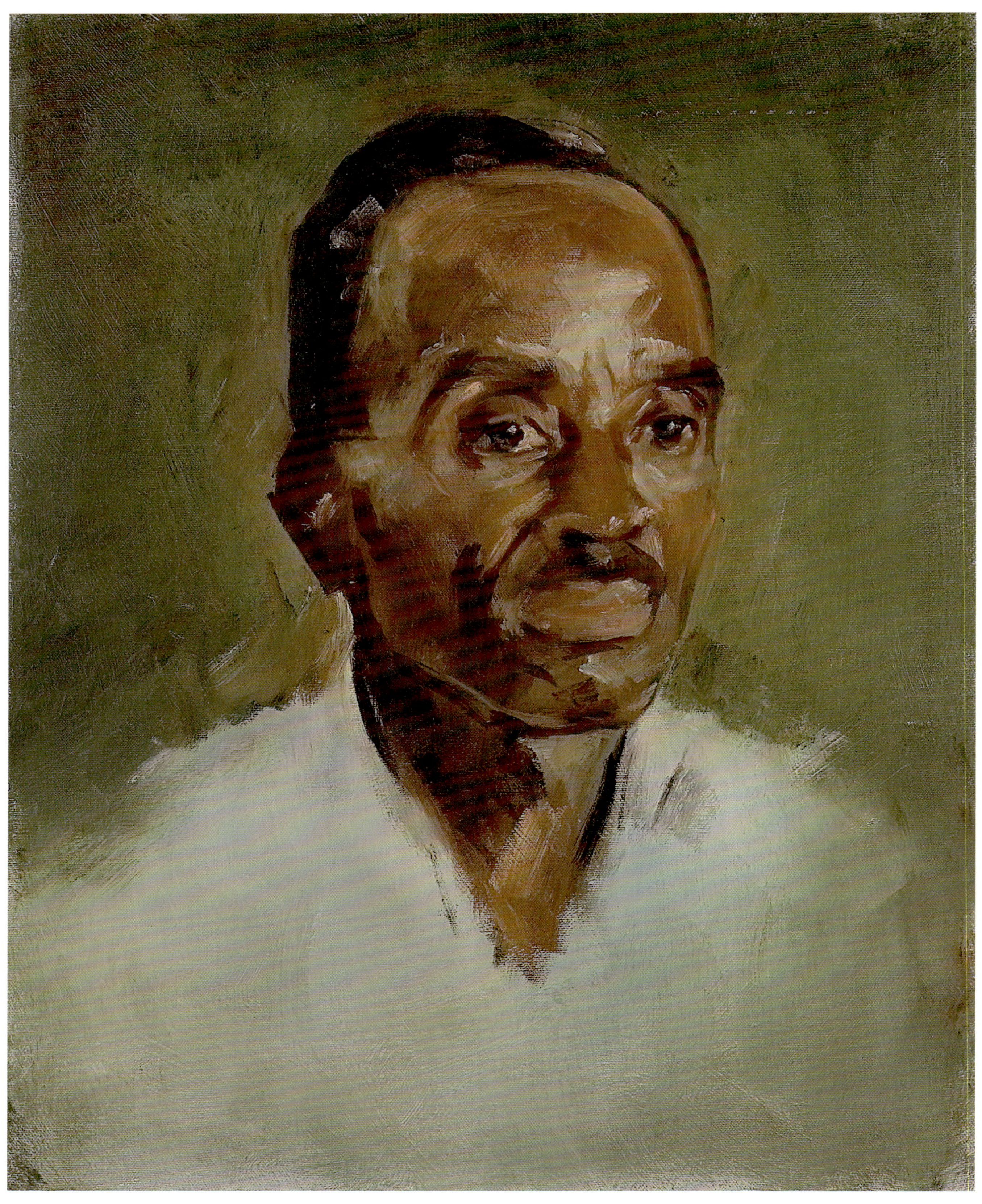

Will Richard, 1979. oil on canvas. 20 x 16.

A Sabbatical from Portraits

I had this month's sabbatical that I could do what I wanted to, and I wanted to paint, say, in the manner of Monet. This was about 1970, I think. The second week I was not too enthused about my painting. The third week I had to force myself to find a tree to paint, and the Monday morning of the fourth week I woke up and I lay there in bed and I said, "I cannot face another tree." So I said, "What do you really want to do in your growth time?" I really wanted to paint a portrait, and so I got the yard man who was working for me in the yard and I said, "Will, sit for me, and we're going to paint a portrait." So I painted a portrait of Will, and I had a wonderful time doing it. I was all alive and I said, "Will, you know what I think? I think this is what God intended for me to do." Then this was proven to me within the last five or ten years—five years I guess—I started getting letters out of the blue from people that I had forgotten names of saying, "Mr. Bouldin how much we've enjoyed your portrait all these years." And I said, "Thank you God, this is what I was meant to do." So anyway what I want to do now I got about, I hope, twenty more years, and I haven't painted that good portrait yet, but I've got about twenty more years to try."

Working with Clients

This is one of the reasons why I'm so interested in portrait painting. You are working for a client. As we start off, you have come to me because you want me to paint your portrait. As they say, I am "zee ar-tizt" but remember, you are my client. I am the artist that is out here to get this thing done in the correct way. Let's say compare myself to a doctor. If you want to have a wart taken off of your nose, I am a surgeon, a doctor; I could go in and surgically take that wart off. But if I know in the back of my mind that it is going to cause your nose to fall off, I better tell you honestly what to do, then you see what to do, and you can see you are on my side. You can see why it won't work. But if I can't tell you why it won't work, it's up to me to change it to make it work the way you want it to work. The reason I use to back that up is I'm trying my best to create a masterpiece. I've never painted a masterpiece before but I'm trying.

I go into a museum, and there are very few real masterpieces in museums, but I really do admire the portraits. They are my masterpieces, because I guess I'm in that field. And I look at it and say, "You know what, this painter had to deal with a client." He had to work for who was going to give him money. He had to please the client and that's my job, and that job hasn't changed. The client had to be pleased in such a way that now that painting is hanging in a museum. But he had the problems that I have.

I always make a color sketch first to show the client, because I learned years and years ago I better show the client what I am doing to prevent a lot of time and heartbreak later. So I paint a little sketch at first of what I'm going to do. In that, I'm going mostly for myself, and it's fine because I know I can tear it up, and in ten minutes I can do another one. I'm very pleased with the little sketch. In fact the lady that commissioned me to do this portrait saw the sketch and said, "I'll buy this," which meant that she's an art lover. But you see I don't have any faith in that sketch because it's all color, movement, and emotion. And she's responding to the emotion. But there's no likeness in the little girl's face, which they want. And knowing this and knowing it's that kind of work, I have to make my portrait to make the art quality that I have in that little sketch. Man, I'm getting closer to getting that masterpiece.

Getting to Know a Subject

The difference between the image of a person and a portrait of a person is you get the feeling of that person with a portrait. And you have to get that feeling [to] come out. Most people do not look at you at all. They know who you are and they store it back there in their mind, they recognize you. Why do they recognize you? Very few people can really describe your physical features. That happens to everybody. Your eyes focus here and focus there, and you really don't look at them all at once. I get this feeling quite a bit. If I've got that feeling of that person in the painting, then I've got a portrait. Sometimes that's very difficult to do. I try to be open with the client from the very beginning. I tell them that you hired me to paint your portrait, and now we've got to get to work. This is going to be work. The first thing I'm going to do is to interview you. I don't use the word interview, but we've got to get to know each other. You've got to know me, and I've got to know you. So it's going to take an hour or two, up to three hours of us being together. So I'll come to town and spend time with you. Usually in that time while we're talking, something will click; it always has. Done. It's the way you put your hand like that and the way you put your thing here that is indicative of you. That will remind the people of you. Sooner or later they get into a position where I see in my mind their personality in that position and I say, "Hold it! Don't move!" I always have an envelope with a pencil in it in my coat pocket. Very quickly I make a stick figure, hand here, this here, I put it where it really means something. Then I tell them that's it. I show them what I've done, and we come to a meeting of the minds. A good portrait is a successful venture between me and you. It's something we both have to cooperate in. You have to work at it and I have to work at it. If we do that, well then we're going to have us a fine portrait. That's the way I approach them.

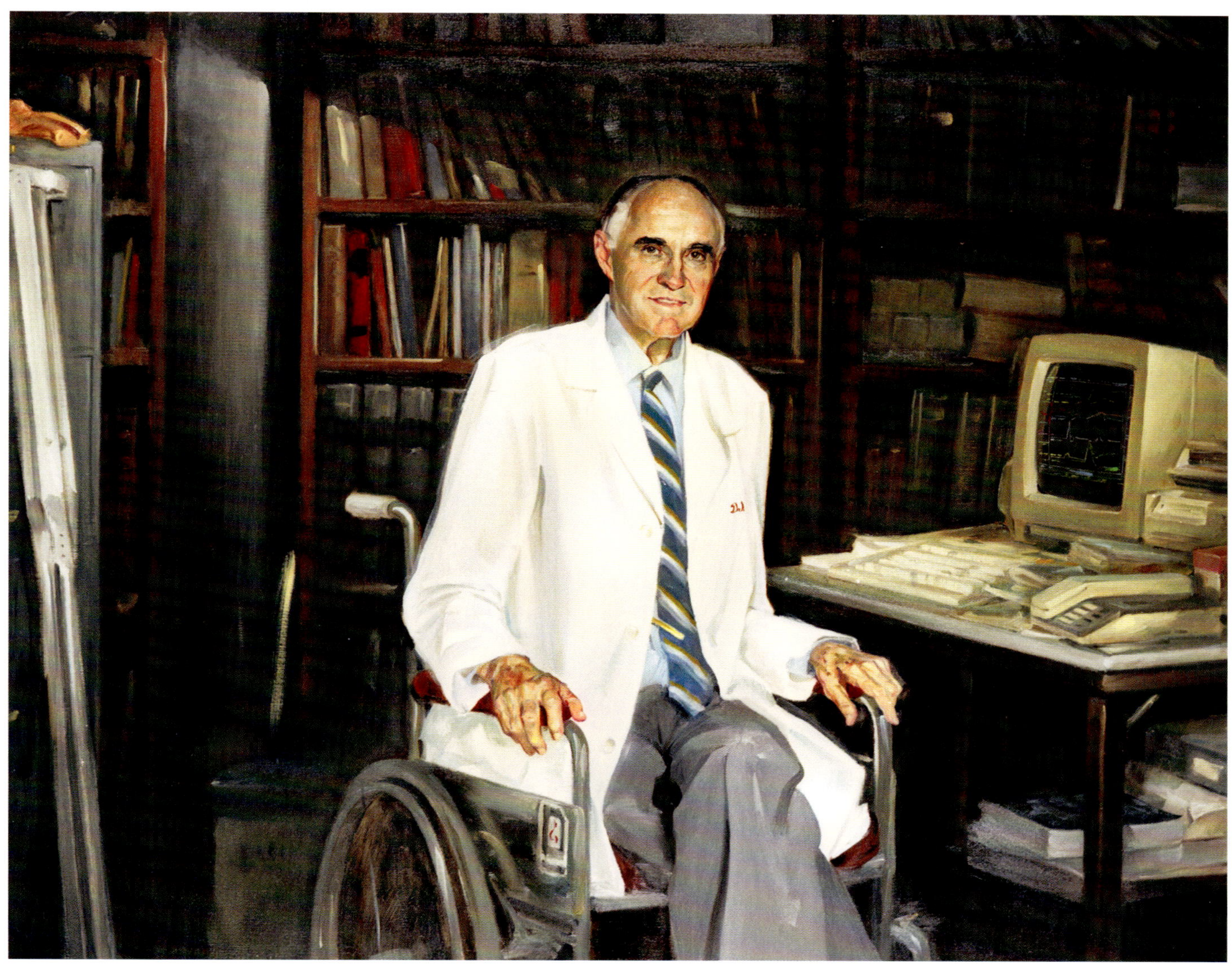

Dr. Arthur C. Guyton, 1993. oil on canvas. 49 x 67. *Collection of the University of Mississippi Medical Center, Jackson.*

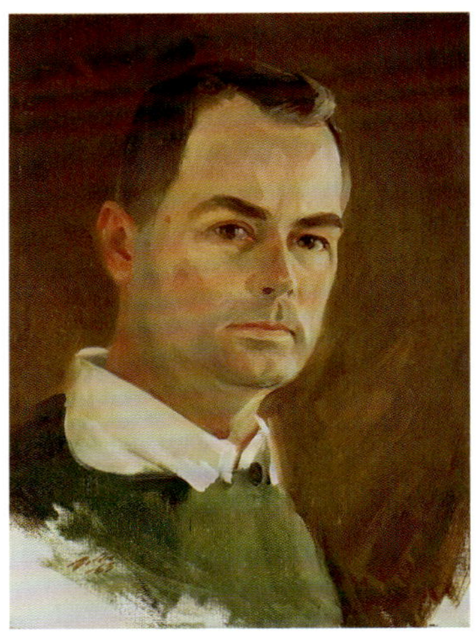

Self-Portrait, 1963. oil on canvas. 18 x 13.

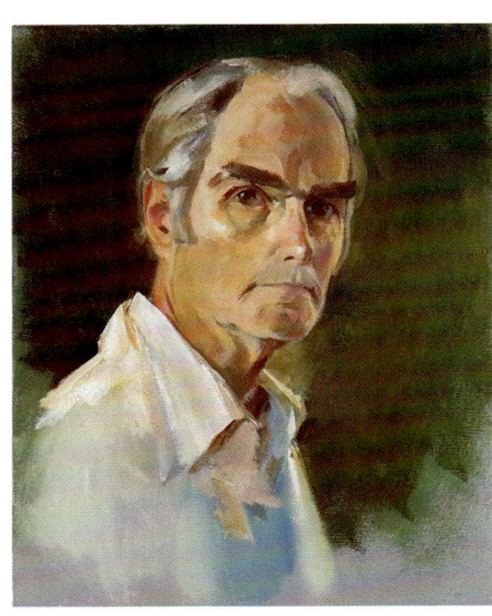

Self-Portrait, 1979. oil on canvas. 20 x 16.

The Spirit of a Portrait

How I learned all this, when I was a young man I thought all artists have beards. I think I'd like to grow a beard, but every time I would try I would chicken out. One time Mel and I were taking a trip to Mexico for about three weeks. I thought that I would grow a beard on that trip. Well I came back with a full grown beard. I walked into her mother's house there, and she did not like the beard. "What, oh, what have you done? I don't like that! Get rid of it. It's awful, just awful," she said. So I just kind of laughed and said that I was going to keep it for a while. Well this whole process led on about three months, and then she stopped talking about it. One day, I was saying that I've got to shave this thing off, but it was a great beard, and I couldn't shave it off. Well I got mad and I went to my paints, and I was having trouble with them. I couldn't do it, and I was crying. I looked at my mirror there in the bathroom, and I saw the beard. I said to that beard, "Ded-gummit a beard dudd'n make an artist! I'm gonna shave you off!" With that I grabbed the razor, and there it went. About that time Mel was flying in airplanes—she flies too! She flew in, and I was out on the strip here on the place. She landed on the runway and got out. She looked up in front of the plane and saw that I had shaved off my beard, said, "No! No! No!" when she stepped out of the plane, "I married a boy!" She liked the beard, you see. I said that her mother disliked this thing so much. Let's not say anything about it and see what she says about it. She agreed. During that last week while Mel was in Memphis, I ate at noon at her mother's house every day for that week. Well, on Saturday, she hadn't said one thing about it. An aunt came by and said, "Oh, Marshall I'm so glad you shaved your beard off." And with that my mother-in-law looked at me and she said, "Oh, you shaved it off! That was the worst looking thing I've ever seen in my life!"

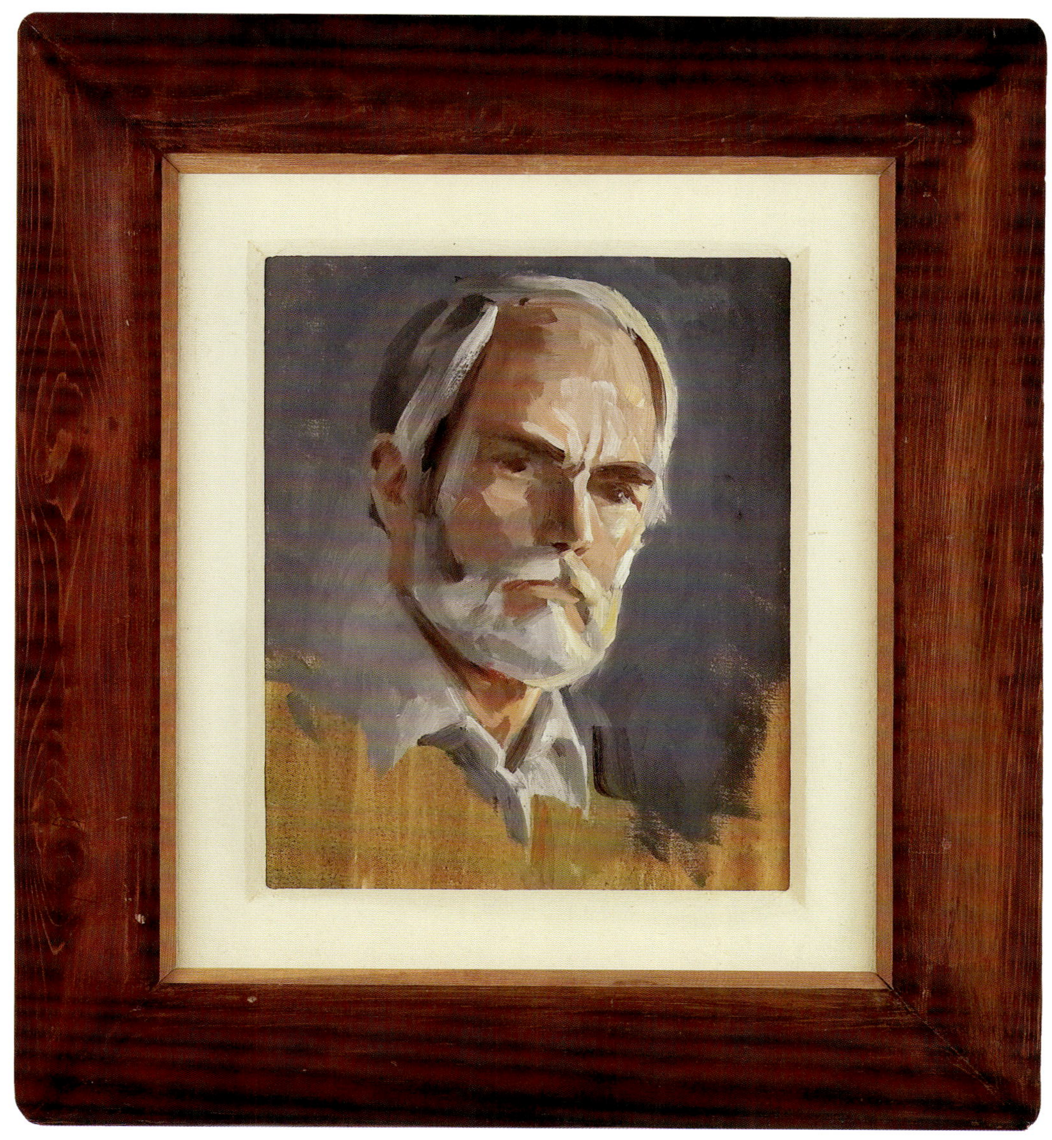

Self-Portrait, 1983. oil on canvas. 16 x 13.

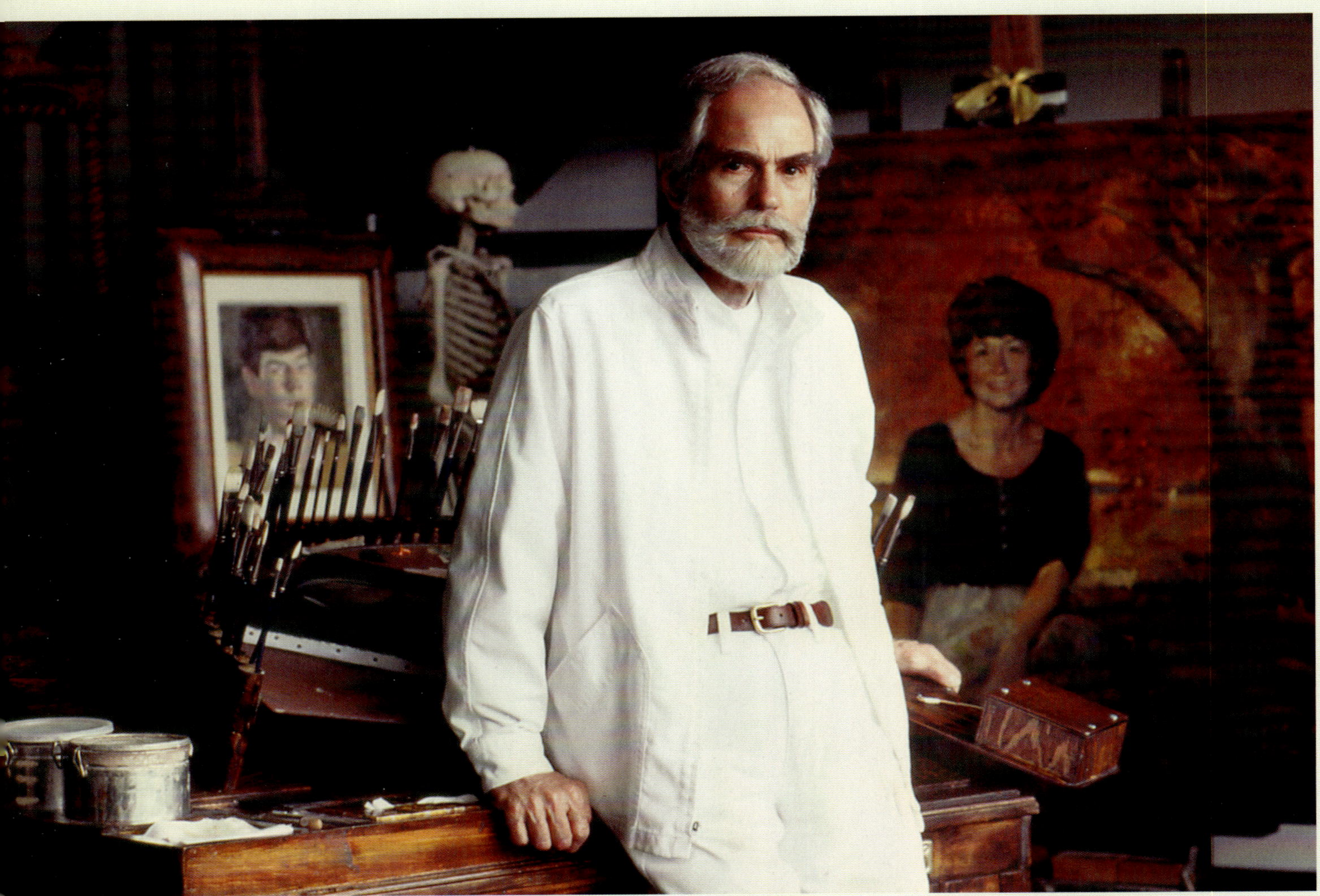

Bouldin in his studio, circa 1986.

I was the same sweet, old son-in-law. The beard didn't make a bit of difference. She didn't even know it was gone. Then I began to think, "You know, I know this person, but which side of the head is their hair parted on?" I don't know which side it's parted on. Then I had another experience with that. I did a lot of self-portraits because I was always available and I always wanted to work from life. Sometimes a friend would come in and say, "Hey! You're painting self-portraits. Well I like that one. I don't like that one, or this one or these." I'd say, "Tell me what's wrong with them." They'd look at it, look at me, look at it for a time and say, "Oh, I know what's wrong with it. The hair is parted on the wrong side of the head."

I'd say, "That's right, but I was painting in a mirror. But what about this painting over here that you like? The hair is still on the wrong side of the head."

They'd say, "Oh, well that looks just like you."

See? So, it's a matter of I had lost my spirit in this other portrait, but I had the spirit of me in this portrait. Then I began to put them all together in my mind, and I got to the point where: people don't really look at you. Here we're getting away from the copied photograph, which is easy to do. You can copy, trace it down, sure that's a portrait and you've got something painted, but if you don't have that feeling you're not going to wind up with something that's a work of art.

A Good Artist

I just believe in God very strongly, and to me it was that I didn't do it. God did it, and I was the vehicle, and that's the way I feel. And man, I just want to be more and more of a vehicle. And you know what, I think that probably I will not ever paint that portrait that I want to paint, and I think probably I will go on into my coffin saying, "A little paint in here with me and maybe I'll paint the ceiling of my coffin!" Isn't that wonderful to have that thought that God has given me a feeling that gives meaning to my life? I tell students they come to me and they want some advice and usually somewhere along the line they will say, "When will I get good?" And it just tickles me to death. I laugh and I say, "Wait a minute, hold it." I say, "Do you know what good is?" They say, "Well..." I say, "Listen, think of it like this: draw a vertical line and up at the top is the best artist in the world who paints good pictures, and here down below is the worst artist in the world who paints pretty bad pictures. Well where in that do you change from being bad to good?" You know, I have watched Sargent go up and down. He's in his grave. I've watched him go up and down in popularity in my lifetime where when I first started, they taught me in school that he was a very inferior artist. Then, in fact, the Art Institute of Chicago didn't show some of his paintings that they had in the basement. When he got popular again, of course he's dead all this time, but when he got popular is about 1980, I think, The Art Institute had a big show of all his paintings, all the paintings that they had in the basement when I was going to school that they wouldn't show, and it just tickled me to death. I said, "Who draws the line? The line moves up and down." So I figured, "Just quit thinking about being good 'cause you'll never get it. You're an artist." Now if you are a commercial type person and you want money, fine. You can work at fame and get it like that. But really, simply painting is what you need to work for. It is not to get good but to have pleasure in it, to enjoy it. So if you are a real artist then the good line is always just a little bit ahead. It's just like a donkey with a carrot out in front of it—you try to get it, and you never get it, and if you do get it you become bored, and do you want to be bored? No.

Excerpted from an interview conducted by Daniel Piersol at the artist's studio, Clarksdale, Mississippi, May 1, 2008.

(Next page) Marshall Bouldin III's Clarksdale, Mississippi, studio soon after its completion in 1967.

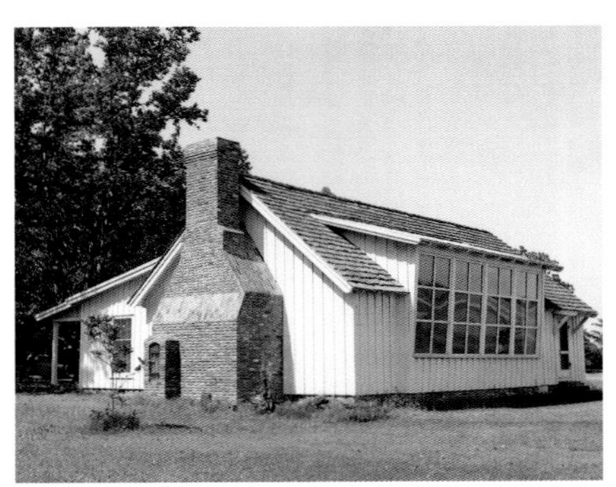